TALES OF DISORDER

BOOK THREE

THE CXNTERBURY TALES

MICK N BAKER

To Chris, Jess and Abbie

For Mum and Dad
With life comes understanding

The Cxnterbury Tales – Book Three
Tales of Disorder

"Patience is a conquering virtue."

-Geoffrey Chaucer

Chapter 1

Punx In Satellites

Punks found it hard living in the satellite towns outside of London. It was a constant struggle, a struggle that began at the start of every breaking day with the hassle we got from our parents, even before we had the chance to spike our hair up or put our bondage trousers on.

One minute you were tucked up in bed dreaming of Siouxsie Sioux, the next, you were in the middle of a total nightmare. It was a war on the home front; parents had woken up to the fact that it wasn't just a fad. It wasn't just going to go away, for most of us it was a way of life, and some of them had had enough of the rebellion; the rebellion may well be televised, but not from their 'bloody front rooms'. It had to be stopped, for our own sakes, and for the sake of what the neighbours might say too, so Maddy and Dummy would try any method to end it, to get their kid back into a society, a society created by them that we thought was boring and pointless.

I thought the whole thing was bullshit, it was like this; what we made, we did it for you, it's all for the best, now get on with it, like it or lump it. I wasn't even going to lump it. No way. I did what I wanted, when I wanted, how I wanted too, and if anybody, any one of society's silly little drones, had the audacity to say no or tried to stand in my way, my reaction would always be the same. Piss off. If that wasn't enough, then OK, I would keep on telling them to piss off until they did, and eventually knowing I would never back down, they did. It was their simple option, the peaceful option, the only way. I was never going to back down; I was a punk rocker.

Once you had got through the parental flak, got yourself outside
onto the streets, the bullshit continued, with the stares and the cheap
comments we got. In the early days of punk, we were just little kids,
and at times it could get quite frightening. So we just took it, stopped
listening, walked on by, thinking. It's better to ignore the idiots, let
them have their silly laughs, but over the years, like the constant drip
of water on solid rock, they got through, started pissing us
off. Punks had changed a lot since the summer of 1977; we had got
bigger, and we had got stronger, angrier. We were ready to react and
more than likely to fight back. It was time, our time to let people
know, we punks weren't going to take it anymore, and if people
wanted to stare, make comments, or worse still, threaten us, then
they were in for a shock; a fucking big one.

Punks around Hertford and Ware I knew, were going through
exactly the same thing I was, and we would meet up, have a few
snakebites, talk it through, find the shared ground, laugh at the
wankers, and make it better. It made us feel stronger that we weren't
alone, knowing we had mates we could rely on when it really came
down to it, people who knew, understood, and I never heard anyone
say that they were going to give in to the bullshit that they had to go
through day after day - they were my mates, they were punk rockers
too.

People soon learnt to leave us alone and give us a bit of respect,
which was a step in the right direction - they gave us room
to breathe - however, we still didn't have anywhere to go. Places that
would let us do our own thing, play our music, so we got bored, and
the bored teenagers started giving trouble to the very people who
had picked on us in the first place.

A couple of pubs in Ware and Hertford who catered for head
bangers, rockers and acid-casualty hippies from the sixties played a

bit of punk now and again, particularly 'Problems' by The Pistols, which was apparently a metal anthem, so we would hang out in them trying to ignore the Bon Jovi, AC. DC heavy playlist. It was somewhere to go, but it wasn't ideal, even though some of the specialist ciders they sold were incredibly moreish. Punks needed a place of their own.

In London, it seemed totally different, and not just because people's attitudes in general were open and more accepting. London had a whole multitude of different cultures, communities, and within those communities there was a punk community. Punk rockers had their own pubs, clubs, record shops, and at the centre of it all, the gigs. Which for most punks was what punk was all about, but for us living out in the satellites, they had been a problem since the early days.

One of us would read about an up-and-coming gig in Sounds, The N.M.E. or on a flyer, tell everyone else about it, so we would all put a few quid by, be buzzing about it for weeks in advance and then on the night of the gig. It would always be the same scenario, we would be standing in the Electric Ballroom or the Lyceum, soaking up the atmosphere, soaking up the snakebites, watching the band, and then when eleven o'clock rolled around and the gig was reaching its crescendo with people going mad chucking themselves about, it was decision time. It was the same question we had been asking ourselves over and over again since our first forays into the capital to go to gigs - should we stay or should we go?

If we decided to go, we would miss all the encores, and walk out of the venue to the sound of the band's best tracks, feeling unnecessarily pissed and necessarily pissed off. Then trudge back to the station to catch the last train home, our only reward being that we would be sleeping in our nice warm beds that night. If we stayed, we would carry on drinking, enjoy the best tracks, join in with the mayhem, and then at the end of the gig, leave the venue with everyone else buzzing, only to find that the last train from Tottenham Hale, our train home, had long gone.

In the summer, the decision was a lot easier; the nights were relatively warm, so it wasn't too bad, it was still uncomfortable trying to sleep on a bench at Tottenham Hale station, but we had seen the whole gig, encores, and all. It just became another part of the adventure. In the winter, the decision became much harder. It was tough going as for reasons known only to the bands - maybe they were having their holidays in the sun - the best ones seemed to play more of their gigs in the winter, which meant an uncomfortable night wriggling around on the unyielding bench slats followed by an early morning hour of hypothermia for us. One morning I woke up shivering from a fitful sleep, to see that my DMs had a layer of frost on them, and my hair had gone solid like a used paint brush, so we would try to find ways to keep the stinging cold at bay.

On one particularly cold winter's night, with Discharge playing at the Lyceum - I knew I wasn't going to leave that one early. So I wore an extra t-shirt, three jumpers and an extra-long coat, over my leather. Which kept me nice and cosy on the way up, then once inside the venue, with no money to check in the extra clothes, I tied the jumpers and coat around me. I thought I had sussed it, but no, it was still no good. I spent the rest of the night bumping into people, like Roland Browning with a tiffin box strapped on his back; and after all of that hassle, once we left the gig and I put all the clobber back on again. I still felt the cold gnawing at my bones when I lay down on my bench at the station. In fact, it was worse than normal. I had got so much hotter at the gig with the extra clothes around me that I was dripping with sweat by the time I left, which froze immediately to my skin when I went outside into the cold night air. I spent the whole night on my bench, feverishly rattling like a hippy smack-head on a sabbatical.

Whiff had a brainwave when we went to a G.B.H. gig a few weeks after seeing Discharge, he reckoned if he got totally legless, then not only would he sleep peacefully on his bench underneath the stars, he wouldn't feel the cold either. Col and the sick boys put up a wall of guitars, while it was fucking whisky time for Whiff and snakebite time for me. We had a great time, and by the time we left, the first part of his plan was evident for all to see. Whiff was totally off his nut. Slurring his words, he told me he loved G.B.F., as he lurched from side to side, in a vain attempt to walk in a straight line. I worked tirelessly, like his guide dog, padding loyally beside him, guiding him around the multitude of obstacles on the underground in between The 100 club in Oxford Street and Kings Cross, trying to avoid a tube disaster.

Once I had navigated our way to the sanctum of Tottenham Hale station, a bleary-eyed Whiff stretched out on his bench and began to emit loud, rasping snores, peacefully disappearing into the land of nod. I watched jealously as he snored his way through the night, and I was thinking of trying it myself the next time; that is, until, I watched him trying to get up off his bench the next morning and found his legs didn't work anymore; they had totally seized up in the night. I soon warmed up; I was laughing so much. It was hilarious. Whiff took ages painfully planting one foot in front of the other, robot-like going up and down the platform, trying to turn the raspberry-slush puppy-like fluid that was flowing in his veins back into blood again.

On the first train of the day, to a backdrop of the rising sun. Whiff admitted defeat, concluding that G.B.H. were brilliant live, but the way he was feeling now, it just wasn't worth it. He reckoned there had to be another way, a way of staying till the end and staying warm. We even discussed the possibility of taking sleeping bags up to Tottenham Hale with us, stashing them somewhere near the station for our next sleep-out. In the end we agreed that it would be a real gamble leaving anything, anywhere in London, no matter how well we hid it, as there were just too many thieving bastards about. If Whiff's one got lifted, his dad, Brian, or Bad Brians as we called him, would be furious as his older, plumb like brother, Talcy Malcy, wouldn't have anything to sleep in, when he did his Duke of Edinburgh's. So the problem remained.

Andy, Whiff and me saw The U.K. Subs, The Ruts, Angelic Upstarts, Sham 69, Cockney Rejects and The Exploited, we also got to see the third wave anarchist punk bands too, Crass, Flux of Pink Indians, Disorder, Chaos UK, Conflict, G.B.H. and Discharge, either missing the end of their sets or freezing our bollocks off, lying slab like on our benches at Tottenham Hale station, shivering, shaking, wearily, waiting for dawn to break, waiting, for the first train of the day to show up, and ferry us back to our houses and our warm beds.

In the summer or winter, warm or cold, we had another problem to deal with, and once again it was something that we had been putting up with from the start. A couple of journeys on the train up to the capital every week could get expensive and divert funds away from more important acquisitions, like snakebite, pouches of old Holborn and the odd visit to Hackney Frontline. So where available, when the opportunity arose, we would bunk the trains, let British Rail take the fiscal strain as well as the logistical. Not only was it a laugh. It was good for my measly post office account balance too, and I found it easy on our quiet branch line, as I had been using the trains for nothing since my incarceration in Richard Hole School.

On the way into Ware station, I would check the bins, find a newish looking, used ticket, then after my journey, walk up to the gate making sure to latch onto a large herd of my 'fellow fare paying passengers' and confidently striding past the ticket inspector, I would flash 'my ticket' at him and he in turn would give it a cursory, 'oh poor me, I'm so over worked' glance and wave me through. I started to believe that I could flash anything at the fat controller and calmly wander through the gate grinning inanely with my funds intact for a night on the snakebite. Over time, I got more and more outrageous with what I flashed at them. I told my mate Danny that I was going to see if I could get through by flashing my arse, and as a fellow fare dodger, he reckoned that if it had a barcode on it, I wouldn't have a problem. I didn't, but I made it through with a Discharge gig ticket, a bus ticket and a coupon for Anchor Butter I pinched from my mum. It was simple, when it came down to it, it was all about front, really. If you looked like you were a well-behaved, fare-paying passenger, then that is what you were.

On a couple of occasions, I nearly got caught, but you could tell the people at the gates and in the ticket offices, couldn't be bothered; they would just give me a warning look and then get back to the sports pages of their newspapers. It would just be more work for them, so for us, the only people to look out for were the ticket inspectors, the ones walking the trains, the ones who were actually paid to check the tickets. Inspectors were a rare sighting, and no real problem as the only station before Ware was Hertford East, so you could see them getting on at the stations on the way up, and as they got on, we would jump off and wait for the next train. It worked like a charm on trains with the separate compartments, and unless you weren't paying attention, and, they got in with you, you would never get caught, and even if you did the fines were punitive anyway. It certainly wasn't going to stop me. I loved outfoxing the dozy bastards; not only was it a challenge, albeit a small one. It was fun, a laugh, and with the money I saved, it meant I could go to more gigs and drink more snakebite. It was win, win, win, win. One thing that always got me though, was no matter how many times Whiff saw me do it, and get away with it, he would never do it himself. He could be quite law-abiding sometimes. Andy, on the other hand, was well up for the suggestion and liked the odd 'Intercity Saver' himself - just like me, he would rather give his money to Bulmer's brewery than to British Rail.

I was totally resigned to the fact that for punks in the satellites, where bands were concerned, it was London or nothing, and then totally out of the blue a solution presented itself. It came completely by chance when Whiff bumped into Dennis 'Dirty Den' Maynard, a hippy mate of his in the Tap, and they had a couple of beers together. It turned out that Dirty Den, had got off the smack for good this time, got off his couch for good this time, and over the weekend he had been to see G.B.H. and wondered why Whiff hadn't been there. Whiff first thought Den had lied about getting straight again, just like all the other times he had given it up for good, as we had seen G.B.H. a few weeks before up in London and told him. Den cackled like an old, toothless crone telling him that he had seen them in Stevenage at a place called Bowes Lyon House. Whiff was gobsmacked, he wanted to know more about this punk oasis outside the sprawling capital, so after buying the always brassic Den a few pints he told the little punk rocker all he needed to know, and a bit more too, and then a brassic Whiff in turn, passed on the good news to us.

Bowes Lyon House in Stevenage was a revelation to us, it was a couple of stops from Hertford North station, so it was easy to get to and even easier to bunk the trains, as there was never any one around collecting tickets at the stations after ten o'clock. Bowes gig tickets were cheaper, as was the beer, and they sold snakebites too, which some other pubs and venues outside of London didn't, apparently, they reckoned it made people go mad, which was why we drank it.

On our second visit to Bowes to see American hardcore band Black Flag, I happened to see a flyer of the last three months gigs, I felt sick as nearly every band we had travelled all the way up to London to see, either missing the end or having an impromptu sleep out at Tottenham Hale station had stopped off at the satellite new town to play Bowes Lyon House. In many cases, it had been on the same tour too. I thought for fuck's sake, all those great encores missed, all those freezing nights on our benches, on the verge of hypothermia, willing our time away, dreaming of our beds, now we really have found our punk rock heaven. We soon became regulars.

Discharge, Crass, Disorder, The Exploited, Conflict, The Subhumans, and UK Subs all played at Bowes, leaving a trail of destruction behind them and us grinning drunkenly in their wake. In amongst the UK's finest third wave punk bands, we saw a relatively unknown Rastafarian punk band from America called Bad Brains, who totally blew us away. It was a real night to remember, they were so fast, so tight, so heavy; and as the floor erupted around them a skinhead decided to gob on HR, their singer, and was warned that 'if you spit you get hit'. A moment later, as the spit left the skinheads grinning mouth, he got hit and soon after left the venue with his tail between his legs, and the indent of HR's microphone on his forehead. It was hilarious.

Punk night after punk night, we had some incredible times over at Bowes and felt that at last we had our own punk rock community; Bowes was our own punk rock central.

One night over at Bowes for another Discharge gig, I jokingly said to Whiff and Andy that we should ask someone if we could play support for one of the bigger bands.

Whiff shrugged his broad shoulders, "Yeah, why not?"

Andy nodded back enthusiastically, "There's no harm in asking, let's do it."

I snorted at the dreamers, watching their leather jacket-studded backs disappearing into another packed house. Yeah, good luck with that, I thought.

Whiff and Andy returned with three pints of snakebite in their hands, big smiles plastered on their faces, telling me that they had left Whiff's contact number behind the bar.

"Cheers, nice one. Here's to a gig at Bowes," I said, picking up my frothy, golden-brown liquid, and I thought we won't be hearing from them again.

*

I knocked on Whiff's door a couple of weeks after Discharge had done the damage at Bowes, and it fell back to reveal a smiling Judy, who welcomed me in. Mick, her black, shaggy-coated Scotty dog came running out yapping, and despite Judy's admonishments, he began to investigate the interesting smells ingrained on my trousers.

Once his inspection was complete, satisfied, he waddled back into the front room, back to his basket near the roaring fire. Judy shouted upstairs for Whiff, but the avalanche of guitars from D.O.A.s album 'Something Better Change' coming down the stairs, emanating from his room, drowned her out.

"It's OK, Mrs. Hammersmith, I'll go up," I smiled.

A roll of her eyes behind her milk-bottle glasses, combined with a face that said, 'I don't know what to do with him', she nodded. I gave her a friendly smile, made my way up the narrow stairs, pushed open his door, and entered the noise. Whiff frowned at the intrusion, like he was expecting his mum to come in on litter duty, but when he saw it was me, he smiled expectantly, so not keeping him waiting, I pulled the little bag of sensi from my leather jacket pocket.

"Yesss… Oh cheers Skin," Whiff said, grinning, "You went then?"

"Yeah, no problems, mate," I said, handing him the goods.

Whiff pulled out his Rizlas and began to stick the three magic papers together. "So, you went to The Frontline? How was it?" He asked.

"It's a battlefield mate," I said, grinning.

Whiff snorted.

"It is mate, no bullshit, it's where the Rastas and the S.S.P.G. go to fight it out, it's the SUS laws, mate, they pull anyone wearing red, gold and green. I mean, OK, from what I've seen so far, all the street dealers are Rastas, but not all Rastas are dealers, everyone gets pulled, even people wearing a Bob Marley t-shirt, well, if you're black."

He nodded sagely and passed me the spliff, "Yeah, I get it, it's out of order mate."

"Yeah, it is, and they'll be more riots soon, most of the people came to the U.K. to make a better life for themselves, not to be oppressed by a bunch of fucking closet Nazi's." I took a lug and tasted only old Holborn. "Oh what, did you actually put any in here?" I asked, reproachfully, blowing on the glowing end, hoping to fire up a bit of sensi.

"Yeah, yeah, yeah," he said defensively, "I thought I'd make a little one."

I snorted, "A little one, I tell you, man, even if you were black Whiff, you wouldn't get nicked by the S.S.P.G. at The Frontline smoking this."

I thought why? Why would anyone make a spliff that doesn't have anything in it? Oh, well, it's his smoke. "It's like cannabis light, mate," I concluded, giving him a confused look.

Whiff laughed, "Ah, it's too early in the day for me Skin, I like stuff that gets me up in the day."

I shook my head, passed the T.H.C.- deficient smoke back to him, and he sat back, viewed his handy work, nodded his head, then took a few shallow puffs himself, blowing the billowing smoke towards the open window, which gently escaped into the clear midday air. In between the last couple of tracks on D.O. A's album the phone began to ring incessantly, from the hall downstairs. I looked to Whiff and a roll of his eyes told me that he couldn't be bothered with any intrusions, so when Judy popped her head around his bedroom door, smiling, telling him that there was someone on the phone for him, I knew what was coming.

"OK, cheers," said Whiff, dropping the smoke into the ashtray, watching the door close behind his mum, "You fucking old slag."

I put my head in my hands, creasing up laughing, he looked around at me, grinning.

"When are you going to stop that, man?" I asked through my convulsive laughter.

"Never… she's a slaaag," He cackled and left.

It was a very quick phone call and when Whiff returned, he was beaming from ear to ear.

"Skin, you are not going to believe this… That was Bowes, they said they were looking for support for The Subhumans after Christmas and would we be interested?"

"Hah, I like it, would we be interested? Nah, we're playing the fucking Albert Hall that night, of course we're interested, what did you say?"

"I said yeah, of course… Skinner, man oh man, this is it, this is the next step for us."

"Yeeessss, that's the best news mate, let's celebrate!"

Whiff picked up his smoke, still beaming.

"Nah, save that one for later, mate, let's have a proper celebration!" I said, pulling out my own bag of sensi, grabbed his papers and started building up.

Chapter 2

Away In a Marina

I thought about the Bowes gig later on, and although it was what we had all been dreaming about since we discovered the place, a few months earlier, playing the gig just after the Christmas holidays wasn't ideal for me for two reasons. One, I was worried about how many people would show up after the season was over, as most people would be skint and or nursing hangovers; and two, Christmas was a strange time of year for me, as I had stopped celebrating 'Christ, our saviour's birthday' when I was fourteen.

In the season to be jolly, while people were out in the pubs drinking and being merry as they had been instructed, I would be doing everything I could to avoid it. I had got fed up with the lies and hypocrisy of it all, the way the Multi Death Corporations used it to push sales up, the way people who normally had no interest or love for the church whatsoever celebrated it so heartily and finally and worst of all; the Christian church, a religion that has caused more deaths than any other ideology throughout history, pushing the idea of peace on earth and mercy mild.

On a personal note, Christmas day was not a great day in the Baker household. It was the day that my richer and better aunt deigned to visit my mum, her lowly and poorer sister, which was not only laborious, it was a complete waste of time, as I don't think anybody really enjoyed the experience. I never knew why they came; it was all so pointless, even with my mum's posh background and the old man's aspirations to be one of the upper class, which was impossible with his harsh, Liverpudlian working-class background, they were poles apart.

Uncle Jack, my aunt's second husband, had retired a rich man after making millions on the futures market, and they had become part of the Surrey jet set. It still wasn't enough. though, what was the point of being rich if you had no power? So when the contract came up to build a new clubhouse at The Frensham Pond Sailing club near Hindhead, Jack pulled a few strings, put in a ridiculously low price, and consequently he got the contract, then surprise, surprise, a few months later, after the completion of the work, even though he had never sailed a boat in his life, he was made chairman of the club and my Auntie Evie made sure everyone knew about that.

Auntie Evie was a serial name-dropper, not only that, a seasoned expert in the art of one-upmanship; it didn't matter how the conversation started or who started it - inevitably, it would always come back to the club and its many famous visitors from around the world. Even when I was a kid, I felt something wasn't right when she 'casually' dropped into a conversation my mum had started about the weather, on how they had almost capsized some 'Lord or Lady?' in their catamaran on their little pond in their Frensham one stormy day, and smiled smugly. I don't know how many times she mentioned that the Sultan of Brunei had visited them on their little pond in Frensham, and he was a lovely man, or that Princess Margaret was 'so very gracious' and Earl Snowden, her then husband, 'smoked too much' and shock horror, he was 'abrupt to one of the waiters' and not forgetting how Peter Sellers 'was so funny when he did his impression of an Indian coolly on a packed-out train from Jaipur to Bombay, when he popped in to their little clubhouse for a drink with his beautiful wife Britt Ekland on his way to the Oscars'.

On and on it went, this not-so-casual name dropping, until eventually, by mid-afternoon, the old man would have had enough of this, quite literally showboating, and would begin operation close down in earnest. Playing his usual trump card, the one that always shut everyone up, the political rant. It would be 'red bastards this', 'Scargill that'. He would rave. He would blame. He would finger point at our now silent guests. Then as the final lap came up on our saviour's day, with evening approaching, everyone would look to the clock, willing Father Time to speed up, get a move on, so the whole sham of Christmas day would be over - for this year anyway.

On the years they brought Derek, their public-school victim of a son along, who in his mid-thirties was like a sort of future version of Doggy; a soul-sapped, hollowed-out, defeated shell of a human being, the inevitable end product of the public school system, it was even worse. Derek, just like Doggy, had been sent to public school when he was around nine years old and for educational enrichment, just like Doggy again, he had been taught to play an instrument, in his case- the violin. Derek's years at Amesbury school had clearly taken its toll on him; he had been encouraged, bamboozled, threatened and in essence, destroyed by his parents' mania for educational achievements and high exam results, so they could impress their rich friends.

I had seen him at my last Christmas dinner, when I was thirteen, and watched open-mouthed, cringing at the vulnerable openness of him as he told everyone, shamefaced, that he had tried out for the string section in the London Philharmonic Orchestra and 'muffed it'. I had burst out laughing at the word 'muffed' as my mate Trotsky, the local expert on lady parts, had told me, it meant minge, and Evie and

Jack had looked at me like I was a beastly, heartless cad, and my laugh froze in my throat, next to a dry piece of Turkey carcass.

Once the little gutter snipe had been silenced, Derek continued in a shaky monotone voice that he was going to 'go into teaching'. On the verge of tears now, Evie went to him, gathering him in, this thirty-three-year-old man and said, 'Oh well if you can't do… Teach' and tittered brightly, quickly adding, 'it will be at a public school, so not quite so bad' and even at the tender age of thirteen, I thought you poor bloke, run away, do anything, but get away as fast as you can.

In the year of my fourteenth birthday, I had stopped celebrating Christmas, so it was no more Auntie Evie and Uncle Jack, or the pathetic wanker Derek for me. When I heard them pulling up outside on Christmas morning, I sought sanctuary up in my bedroom, where I would spend the whole day in peace on earth and mercy mild, listening to music, smoking roll ups and blowing the smoke out of the window, until thankfully at around nine o'clock, they would get back into their jag and piss off back to Slurry.

Once I started using the pubs regularly, it became more difficult to avoid the festivities, so I just treated the Christmas weeks like every night was either a Friday or a Saturday night, as that was what it felt like. In the two weeks leading up to New Year's Eve The Anchor was absolutely packed out with revellers. It was an incredible sight; some older regulars had even brought their wives along with them, many of whom we had never seen before.

In amongst the usual crowd of youth club members, there was Mac, Simmy, Andrew 'wonky eye' Wainright, with his wife, Smiley Sue,

Dale Colins, and his girlfriend Ruth 'Rocky Balboa' Swift. David 'Sid' Crane, his girlfriend Jill and Kevin 'King of the Blockheads' Green whose corner thankfully wasn't chipped off, despite Dr Dave's early diagnosis. Seb Harrington, who somehow knew about us pissing in people's drinks at Tarnia Gorden's party and cracked me up by taking his pint to the bogs with him when he needed a piss, 'to be on the safe side'. Reg Cooper, Bob Williams and Colin Hill all came in for a few pints and one night told us that Pigman Cannon would be making an appearance and seeing the shocked look on our faces, creased up laughing. Lee and Glyn showed off their new girlfriends, Laura 1 and Laura 2, which confused everyone, as the older Laura was going out with the younger Walker. I saw Gobber a few times, who for some reason kept on asking me if he could join the band. On the fourth time of asking, I had had enough, so I told him if he learned how to play Theremin, we would let him join, and encouraged, he went off to find out what one was. Mark and Cerys came in with Gobber, Mark was friendly again, and I soon understood why, as Cerys was monosyllabic, well off with me and obviously still pissed off with my, off my nut version of 'It's Fucking Whisky Time' by Bulldozer, particularly the over-the-top choreography down at the pavilion all those months ago.

Phil was in most nights, too, on great form; he still reckoned that Dave and me owed him a few pints after almost being run over by Hilary Charman, our local psychopathic vicar, which was probably true, as it was our fault, so we kept his pint glass topped up whenever we saw him. It was always money well spent as Phil never stopped making us laugh. Richard 'Ronnie' O'Keef and his girlfriend Julie, showed up with her mate Sammy, more commonly known as 'Ski Sunday' around the village as now and again when it took her fancy, she used to take Mal "'a la" Tete and Coops out into the countryside, find somewhere quiet, lie down in between them, unzip them and start skiing. I saw Danny, whose eyes shone red for most of the two weeks, and as always, Taddy and Craig, who had just about moved into The Anchor by then.

*

On New Year's Eve, I was sitting in one of the snugs in the packed-out main bar, with Lucy flat Chesterman, Brother Vincent, Seb, Mal "'a la" Tete, Coops and Ski Sunday. Next to us the pubs open fire blazed, keeping the winter chill at bay, and we were all beginning to relax, open up, enjoy the atmosphere of The Anchor in seeing out the old year and welcoming in the new one.

Ski Sunday sunk her vodka and orange, slammed the glass down on the table, wiped the back of her hand over her full glistening red lips and turned to me, smiling as the heat of the voddy spread, "I saw my mate Karen yesterday, Skinner, she was talking about you, talking about Sally's party in Ware, you remember that?"

"Karen who?" I asked, smiling lewdly.

Ski Sunday brayed loudly and punched me on the arm, "Oh you. You know exactly what I'm talking about it was so funny, Sal's dad coming in and catching you two at it."

"Yeah, it was hilarious, we were in his bed, he was fuming," I said, rubbing my now-throbbing arm, "Where did you see her? I bet she was out on the piss."

"No, no it wasn't," she said, looking at her empty glass, then to Coops, who gave her a nod, before disappearing to the bar, "I saw her at the family planning clinic."

I gawked at her, my mind racing going back to the night in question, thinking, did we, do it? Did we? No, we didn't; a wave of relief passed over me. No. Definitely. Not.

Ski Sunday threw her back, laughing,

"Ooh, my word, your face is a picture, no you're OK, she said, she only gave you a blow job"

I carried on gawking, my mind racing, going back to the night in question, thinking, did she? No, she didn't; a wave of disappointment passed over me, no she didn't.

Ski Sunday laughed some more, punched my shoulder, making it ache all over again, "Oh you, no, you're safe, she's been a very naughty girl, has Karen, she told the bloke she was with, she was on the pill when she wasn't, she wants to get pregnant; she says if she gets pregnant the council will have to give her a flat, then she can get away from her bitch of a mum for good."

I stared at her, didn't know what to say. I was totally dumbfounded. "Oh what, Jesus fucking Christ, er, oh my fucking … Well, congratulations to you though, Ski, er. Sammy, when's yours due then," I blurted out, and picked up my pint for a much needed drink.

Ski Sunday gave me a withering look, "It's not, it won't be. I was at the family planning to talk about getting an abortion."

I choked on my pint, slowly put my glass down on the table, and looked around at the others.

Ski Sunday creased up laughing, "Oh you, you are so funny, I know why Karen likes you … I'm off for a piss, I'll see you in a minute boys."

Mal "'a la" Tete rolled his eyes at me. I gave him a tight smile back, and in the silence that followed I looked over his shoulder to the opening pub door and saw Hayley Williams come in with Aaron Thornhill, a notorious Teddy Boy, punk basher from Watton at Stone and a regular at the pub where Jamie 'the Whiff basher' Duggan had been shot.

Oh shit, what the fucking hell is he doing here, I thought, and he's with Hayley too. I bobbed down behind Mal, hoping she wouldn't see me, but too late, she saw me alright. She waved happily, then dodged a couple of worse-for-wear people by the door, and began weaving her way through the rest of the revellers towards our snug, and I started looking for the nearest exit.

Hayley smiling face appeared above Mal's shoulder, "Oh hello, Skinner, you're not trying to hide from me, are you?"

"Nah, nah. I've, er, got a gnat bite on my leg, I was just scratching it. It's driving me. Mad," I said feebly, holding her eyes, not daring to look what The Ted's face might be doing.

Hayley laughed, shook her blonde locks, "Aaron this is David's friend, Skinner."

"You alright, Skinner," he said, pulling a big smile onto his face, reaching out a huge paw, "Listen, Hayley said you were OK, so if she says you're OK, then you're OK, as far as I'm concerned… All that stuff between The Teds and The Punks is finished I don't know why it started in the first place… It's in the past, it's all history."

I looked at his shovel-like hand, glanced at Hayley, who smiled thinly, nodding her head, so I took it, shook the huge Ted's hand and as we broke, he crunched my fingers just to let me know he had other options.

"Alright Aaron," I said.

"Oh, you know each other then?" Queried Hayley.

Aaron and me grinned at each other.

I said, "Yeah, sort of."

Aaron smiled broadly, flourishing a thick wad of tenners, "So what you having then, Punk Rocker?"

"Err… OK cheers Aaron, I'll have a snakebite," I replied, flabbergasted, still not quite believing what was happening.

Hayley sniggered and looked at Aaron, "You sure you don't want a whiskey, Skinner?"

Aaron chuckled, "It's fucking whisky time!"

I thought, fucking hell is there anyone who doesn't know about that, "If I do, I might have to drop my trousers again," I quipped, making light of it.

Hayley fell onto The Ted's broad shoulders as they both cracked up laughing.

"You want the usual Hayley?" Asked Aaron.

Hayley nodded in the affirmative, sat down and Aaron headed off for the bar.

"So, where's Dave then? I saw his van lit up by the Christmas decorations in the car park," I asked Hayley as she got comfortable.

She laughed, "Oh yes, I saw that very Christmassy... Stewart's gone mad this year, hasn't he?"

"Stewart's mad all year," I said, "Where is Dave, though?"

She frowned. "We won't see him tonight, he's around Steph's."

"Oh what? Is he not dropping in for one?"

Shaking her head, she said, "No, sadly not Skinner."

I thought great, then a snakebite appeared next to me, chasing away my blues.

Aaron said, "There you go, mate, good health to you." Squeezing in between me and Hayley. He raised his pint, "To Elvis Presley!" He said scrutinizing me, testing The Punk.

Oh well fuck it, I thought here we go, bye, bye cruel world. "To Sid Vicious!" I parried.

Aaron laughed at the front of the cheeky little Punk Rocker, touched my glass with his, "Yeah… Both Rockers, both gone, both not forgotten."

Aaron and me both took a long draft, which I probably needed more than him, as my throat had been parched since he had walked in. Aaron sighed, wiping his mouth as he lowered his pint and I noticed his drink was a strange shade of purple and congealing like blancmange.

"What you drinking there?" I asked.

"It's an old Teddy Boy's drink called Black Witch," he replied, adjusting the gleaming bovine head on his boot-lace tie.

I picked it up, observed the snakebite like build-up of sediment at the bottom, I guessed, "Cider, lager and black?"

"Cider, lager, Pernod and black," He corrected.

"Jesus, that sounds lethal… I'll have a some of that!"

Nodding his head, he said, "Good lad."

Once The Black Witches had been served up, The Ted and The Punk settled back with Hayley and the others for a proper session. Hayley sometimes steering the conversation away from my seething hatred for the Elvis copyist wanker, Shakin' Stevens, who for some reason was riding high in the charts with 'Green Door'. I couldn't have given a flying fuck what was behind his Green dooooooraah, I thought the track had come out of his brown door.

25

On the countdown to midnight, I looked around me at the smiling, happy, pissed-up, faces in our snug. Craig, Taddy, Hayley, Aaron, Ronnie, Ski Sunday, Coops, Mal and Seb, glasses raised up, saying goodbye to the old and bringing in the new. I thought this is going to be our year; it's our time, and although I was happy, I wondered where the rest of the band were, the people who were going to join me on Virus V1's journey into this unknown new year. A roar of excitement built up in The Anchor, the chimes rang out from Big Ben and 1982 turned into 1983. Poppers launched streamers high into the air, whistles blew, people jumped up, shook hands, pats on backs, cuddles, and kisses exchanged. In our snug we all cheered, revelling in it, laughing carelessly, throwing our spilling glasses together, welcoming the new year in, with a big splash of alcohol. I thought this is the real heavenly peace, a New Year's Eve with a group of your mates in your local, not in some stale, dusty old church surrounded by the remains of the long dead.

It wasn't over yet either, Stewart the landlord called a lock-in at midnight, which in effect turned The Anchor into a private party with us being his guests, we still had to pay though, as Stewart's New Year's Eve spirit didn't run that far, but nobody cared, as we were all too pissed, we just got stuck in, got our heads down and tried to drink his pub dry.

In the wee small hours of the new year, about two, I said goodbye to my assembled mates and ignoring the lewd 'I'll see you outside look' from Ski Sunday, much to the relief of the circling Coops and Mal, I shakily made my way to the door, only to find Danny blocking my way.

"What are you doing, man?" I said reproachfully, rocking backwards.

He grinned, "I've got something to show you, Skinner."

"Oh yeah? What is it? If it's your limp worm like dick, you could ask Ski Sunday to take a look, I bet she'd take you out on the white run, if you want, there might be a queue though."

Danny gawked at me, confused.

I crooned, tunefully, "The swords of a thousand men." Sniggering manically, not giving a shit if anyone heard, in fact, hoping people heard it was so funny.

Danny cracked up laughing,

"Ooh, Aah, Ooh Aah… Ay," he crooned back.

Danny looked back into the pub, eyeing up Ski Sunday, weighing up his options, then seeing Simmy latching onto the threesome of Coops, Mal and Ski Sunday, he thought better of it, two's company, three's a crowd, but four is downright unsanitary, his face seemed to suggest. He had other things on his mind anyway, so he gestured for me to follow him and we left the pub, out into the cool New Year's Day early morning air, and made our way around the side of the pub, where I saw Phil, his face pressed up against the wall, balancing, mumbling to himself.

"You alright Phil?" I asked.

Phil burped back sickeningly, in my direction.

"Yeah, Happy New Year, man," I said absently, "OK, so what's this surprise then Danny, you got any puff or what?"

"No, sorry, it's all gone, isn't it, Phil?"

"What? Isn't it Phil, what?" Asked Phil, from somewhere very far away.

Danny placed his hands on Phil's shoulders, turned him away from the wall, and steered him in the direction of the car park at the back of the pub.

"Come on, Phil, let's go," Danny encouraged.

Phil waddled, duck-like onto the gravel car park, hands out at his side like a kid playing airplanes, crunching towards the festively lit-up AD Marina van nestling peacefully at its edge. Danny, and me at his side helping, shepherding him along.

"Is he alright to drive?" I stated.

Phil rounded on me sharply, almost going over, "I'm fine, Skinner."

"Fine," he repeated to himself, chuckling, liking the sound of the word.

I liked the sound of the word too. "Yeah, you're fine," said I.

Danny waved away any doubts on the matter, saying conclusively: "Fine, fine, he's fine."

Phil spread his arms out again, his bleary red eyes trying to focus on the little yellow Marina van, basking in the lights from the surrounding Christmas trees, Father Christmases and various nativity scenes, and he sang, "Away in a Ford Marina, no place for a bed, the little lord Skinner laid down his sweet head."

I snorted, "Cheers Phil, that was beautiful,"

"Cheers I love you guys," he said, walking on, and he tripped over an extension cable.

"Aoooooaaaghhhhh," he said, his face flat on the ground.

I looked to Danny.

"He's fine," he said.

"Yeah, he's Fine, fine," I echoed back, as we picked him up, dusted him down, and once he was pointing in the right direction, we helped him over to the lit-up Marina van.

Phil pulled the keys from his pocket, thrust them jauntily into the lock and began rotating them left, right, left up, scratching at the paintwork on the door; eventually the lock popped, the van opened, and we piled in with me taking shotgun, while Danny hopped in the back.

"OK, come on then Danny, where are we going? What's this surprise?"

"You'll see, you'll see!"

I thought, I don't know why he's bothering, it's probably a bit of that squidgy black that Del's been knocking out, it's good shit that stuff, if that's it I'm more than… A sharp blast from the van's horn disturbed me from my thoughts, making me jump in my seat, spinning around, I saw that Phil's head was flat on the steering wheel, tongue lolling.

"OK Phil, come on, stop fucking about, let's go!" I said, trying not to laugh at the maniac.

Phil creased up, lifted his head back up and Hilary-ed, "I've got a bucket of worms and pail of piss for you, Baker, a bucket of pail and a worm of piss, for you, I tell you,"

"Come on, Phil, let's go... Now, fucking hell!!!" I scalded him.

"I'm fine, I'm fine, fine." He told himself as he leant forward in his seat, pushed the key into the ignition, slotting it in effortlessly.

Phil turned the key in the ignition with another deft flick and at once the van came to life, his grinning teeth shining over at me. He put it into gear, looked over his shoulder, checking behind-and I glanced too, making doubly sure he didn't go anywhere near the other two cars that sat in the quiet car park. One of which was Stewart's lime-green Ford Capri, his pride and joy.

Phil revved the engine, savagely, lifted his foot off the clutch, and the van charged forward into a huge spruce Christmas tree, over two reindeers, flattened the three wise men at the edge of the nativity scene, and stopped just short of the little lord Jesus' sweet head.

In front of our shocked, gaping faces, the last upright Christmas tree blinked off, blinked on, blinked off, on, then it toppled backwards with a loud crack, which echoed around the car park.

I heard an eerie buzzing sound, like strangled electricity coming from underneath the van; then there was a flash, another crack and all the lights in the car park went out.

"You fucking Grinch, Phil!" Said Danny, sending us into fits of laughter.

"Jesus Christ! Phil!" I shouted.

Phil grinned to himself, "Oh shit, I think I've blitzed Blitzen."

"You've blown Jesus away in a manger, you fucking Grinch," Danny quipped.

"Listen, we'll be the ones getting fucking blitzed and blown away if you don't get us the fuck out of here, we need to go now," I told them, sobering up quickly, hating it.

"OK, OK," Phil replied petulantly. He began frantically twirling the gear stick around like he was stirring a bowl of soup, eventually finding the correct gear- reverse, he tentatively reversed out, raking back over the festive debris, which clawed, pulled, scratched at the bottom of the van.

Once we had cleared the Christmas carnage, Phil chucked it into first, pulled down hard on the steering wheel, swung the van around the car park, pitching me hard against the door, and we headed for the exit, then raced out onto Anchor Lane, heading for safety.

"Oi you fucking bastards!" Someone bellowed from an open window in the pub.

Danny's head poked into the front of the van. "It's Stewart, go, go, go!" He shouted, panic rising in his voice.

Phil stamped down hard on the accelerator, throwing the van forward, pushing us back into our seats, and we screamed off down Anchor Lane in first gear, doing about thirty miles per hour.

I could hear something else, a grinding sound was coming from underneath the van, "What the fucking hell's that noise Danny?" I said, wondering what the fuck was going on now.

"I don't know, it's coming from the back. I'll check it out."

Danny's head disappeared into the back of the van, then suddenly there was crack, a loud bang and the van lurched forwards, lifted and then bumped down again.

"I think we took a Christmas tree with us, it's just dropped off, it's on the road behind us," Danny howled, descending into hysterics.

"Phil mate, Danny's right about you, you're a fucking Grinch, that Christmas tree is well fucked," I joked, sending Danny into fits in the back.

"Yeah, what have you got to say about that, Grinch?" Came from the back.

"I'm fine, fine," said Phil, convulsing with laughter, and he took a juddering left onto the A10, steering the van in the direction of High Cross Hill, the engine still protesting but not as much, now that we had jettisoned our nativity scene ballast.

"Danny, Pigman Cannon's lives in High Cross, so listen, if
this is about hassling Cannon in his sty, I'm not interested mate, I
can't be bothered, I'm too pissed. It's the season of good will to all
men, and pigs too… Er… Probably."

"Skinner, you know me too well, don't worry, there's no risk… It's
just a bit of sightseeing, cultural sightseeing, trust me, you're going to
love it," said Danny, his head popping back into the front over my
shoulder.

I shook my head, thinking, what have I got myself into now? Oh,
well, I shrugged my shoulders and turned to the more pressing
matter of Phil's driving. Phil's face was a picture of concentration, he
was now doing thirty-five miles an hour, and the engine had stopped
screaming, it was actually pleading now.

"Other gears are available, mate," I encouraged.

"Oh yeah," he said, vacantly.

Phil swung his foot out, depressed the clutch, sending us all lurching
forwards, pulled the gear stick backwards, fumbled it sideways. The
gear box let out a horrible crunching noise, telling him that there was
no way through, so he rammed it forwards, then back again
and finally, after freewheeling for the best part of ten seconds, he
struck gold, we were in second.

"He's fine, fine," Danny said, cackling in the back and just to prove
it, Phil changed up into forth just as we hit the bottom
of High Cross Hill and the van started to complain all over again.

Only this time it was a different kind of complaining. Instead of the high-pitched screaming, it was a low rumbling grumble as the engine struggled in the high gear to make progress on the steep gradient of the hill, and the gradient was increasing by the second.

"Phil mate, you need to change down mate," I told him.

Phil let out a huge, deflated sigh, "It was change up, now it's change down, you're never happy, are you Skinner? Go on then tell me what to do, I'm all gears,"

"Oh, good one, just change down you dickhead… Or Alan will find his fucking gearbox in the middle of the A10 tomorrow morning."

Phil looked a bit hurt, huffily obeying my request. "No, you're alright, Skinner," he said laughing, and Hilary-ed, "Unlike that hypocrite Williams, if that hypocrite Williams, comes around my house again, he'll be for it, I'll give him short shrift, I'll tell you that for nothing… I've got a bucket of piss and a pail of worms waiting for him, a pail of piss, you can rely on it… Or any other miscreants, for that matter." Chortling manically to himself.

Once we had finally summited High Cross Hill, Danny said, "OK, Phil pull into the garage."

Phil chortled, "What that one there next to Cannon's place?"

"Yeah," said a laughing, Danny.

I turned to him, "Oh, for fucks sake, Danny."

"Skinner, trust me!"

I nodded, uncertainly. I thought, I don't believe a single word you
say, mate, but I'm too pissed to care right now. So I sat back
powerlessly, the passenger that I was, watching as Phil pulled the van
off the main road, and reversing surprisingly well, he parked up
underneath a billboard at the side of the garage, still keeping the
engine running.

"OK, get out and check the billboard," Danny urged.

I surveyed Cannon's house opposite warily, saw there were no lights
on, saw it was all quiet on the sty front, so I cautiously
opened the door and peeked up at the billboard.

On top of an advert for Duckham's Multigrade Oil, super-imposed
in white spray paint, it said in huge two-foot-high letters, PC
CANNON MAKING BACON, underneath there were two pig
heads, one on top of the other looking down at me grinning. I
screwed my eyes up in the glare of the garage forecourt lights to get a
better look, and saw that the two pigs seemed to be shagging. Yeah,
they were shagging alright, the one on top, which was sweating
profusely, drips everywhere, had P.C. Cannon's thick eyebrows, tell-
tale moustache and was giving the sow below him a proper pounding
with his corkscrew-like dick.

I fell onto the bonnet of the van, my body convulsing with laughter,
closely followed by the others.

"Oh, fucking hell, that's amazing, Danny, who did that?" I
yelled, wiping the tears from my eyes.

Danny held up his white-spattered hands, "Me and Phil did, about
an hour ago."

"Oh what, he's already driven up here?" I said, incredulously.

Danny and Phil's eyes twinkled back at me.

I put my hands up quickly, knowing full well what was coming next. "Yeah, yeah, I know he's fine, fine," I said, sending us back into hysterics again.

Danny turned his attention back to his masterpiece, scratched his chin studiously, "If you stand back a bit, you can get a better feeling of the work."

"Lovely brush work," slurred Phil assuredly.

I stood back, took it in and proclaimed, "Danny mate, it's a triumph, another proud moment in the village's history, we've seen sunflowers by Van Gogh, the Haywain by Constable, now we have PC Cannon Making Bacon by O' Shea."

"Cannon's a cunts-tble," said Phil groggily. "A chief cunt's-tble… Morning chief cunt's table… What's a cunt's table?" He added, rambling.

I smirked, "I don't know Phil, but I reckon Cannon sits at its head."

"I'm a chief cuntzzzz table, evening all," Phil rambled on, bending his knees going up and down.

"OK Phil, we get it, mate," I said, turning back to Danny, rolling my eyes.

Danny said, "I would love to see his snout when he opens his curtains first thing tomorrow morning." Cracking up.

"What a start to his year, the little piglet… Happy New Year, Tamworth," I said, opening the van door, hoping to get out of here before the sty awakened.

"Morning cunts-tble," said Phil.

"OK, come on, James Hunt," I said, to the still rambling Phil, "Take me home and don't spare the gearbox."

"He won't!" Said Danny, opening the back up and piling in again.

Phil took about twenty minutes to do the five-minute journey back to mine, and on the way, he must have left about half of the unfortunate Marina's gear box on the road behind us, once back at mine, I threw the door open, jumped out, I couldn't get out quick enough.

"Happy New Year lads," I said, happy to be safe, back on terra firma again.

Danny jumped into the front next to Phil, both of them wishing me the same, and after one stall, the van kangaroo-ed off up the road and disappeared around the corner. I went around the back of my house, fumbled my keys out of my pocket, put it into the lock, and almost fell through the door into the kitchen, where I found the old man waiting for me, sitting at the table.

"OK, put your dukes up!" He said, jumping up, taking a Queensbury-rules-type boxing stance.

"What's your name? John Wayne?" I replied aggressively putting 'my dukes' up, trying to focus on him as he bobbed and weaved.

"I'm not being serious; I'm just pulling your leg. I wanted to know if you're a peaceful drunk or an aggressive one."

"You know I'm not into violence, Dad," I replied, sitting down heavily.

"I know. I know. Hey, I'm hungry, do you fancy some cheese on toast with me? It'll soak up some of that alcohol."

I was surprised by his benevolence and not just a little bit hungry too, so I nodded my head, "OK cheers, that would be good Dad." And he set to work.

The old man took the bread out of the breadbasket, began cutting it, "I know I don't know much about the pop world, but I've been thinking about it and I'll say this to you… Be careful of the groupies, they are riddled with gonorrhea and syphilis."

I creased up laughing, he protested, "It's a fact, it's a fact!"

I smiled to myself, thinking, are you pulling my leg again? Oh well, he's only trying to help. "OK Dad, yeah, I'll mind the groupies," I replied, to mollify the old boy's concerns.

He nodded his head, satisfied that he had just spared me the agony of the disease, as he cut up some cheese, placed it onto the bread, put it under the grill, and we sat back.

"I'm thinking of retiring this year, what do you think?" He asked, suddenly.

I was totally taken aback by that question, he never talked about his feelings or personal life with me, ever, let alone asked for my advice. It was so unlike him, I didn't know what to say, usually he'd be the one giving me advice, advice I didn't need, lecturing me about something that I didn't need to know about, or ranting about some politician I didn't want to know about.

"Yeah, it's a good idea," I said, eventually.

He pulled an amused look, "I thought you might say that, yep, I'm going, I've done forty-five years as a P.A.Y.E slave, now I want some time for myself."

I nodded thoughtfully, still not quite sure what had just happened.

A huge smile spread across his face, "Oh look who's here, he's come to wish us a Happy New Year!"

I followed his gaze and saw our cat George's white face at the door.

"Hey, let him in, Mike, he loves a bit of cheese on toast, he plays give me paw with me," he said, smiling broadly at his little pal through the wired glass.

I snorted, "No, that's dogs, Dad." I told him, opening the door, and watched the little ginger and white cat leg inside out of the cold night air.

"Dogs and clever cats, come on boy," he said, and not for the first time that early New Year's Day morning, I thought, are you pulling my leg, Dad?

Once the cheese on toast was ready, the old man slapped the two pieces onto a plate, brought them over to the table, giving me a piece and taking one for himself. I took a couple of bites and started feeling better straight away, then he patted his hand gently on the chair next to him.

"Come on then," he beckoned, looking down at his miracle cat.

George looked up at him coolly, wondering what this two-legged cat wanted.

"Come on then, gimme-paw, gimme-paw," the old man explained, reading his mind.

George's eyes flashed as the penny dropped, making a dooting sound to announce his arrival, he effortlessly leapt up onto the chair, circled, sat down and looked at him expectantly.

"I don't believe it," I said.

"You t'aint seen nothing yet!" He replied. "Gimme- paw," he said, putting out his hand.

George offered out his right paw, the old man gave it a firm, business-like shake.

I laughed, "Whoa, that's amazing, do it again!"

The old man laughed, "No problem."

He took a small piece of cheese on toast between his thumb and forefinger and showed it to George, who's eyes immediately latched onto it.

"Gimme-paw."

George's paw zipped forward, and the two pals shook on it again.

On and on it went, until he noticed his dwindling supply of cheese on toast.

"Bloody hell, look at that, the little bugger, he's eaten all of my grub," he said, staring at George accusingly.

George nonchalantly held his gaze, blinked at him a couple of times, then swivelled his head back to the old man's now nearly empty plater, hoping.

I laughed, "I'm living with Doctor Doolittle."

He chuckled, "OK Mike, look, Happy New Year, I'm going up to my stinking flea pit now."

"Happy New Year Dad, see you, I won't be long."

He got up to leave, then stopped, put his hand on mine, patting it. "And good luck with your pop concert," he said with a smile, leaving George and me in the kitchen with the last bits of my cheese on toast.

I reached out, "Gimme paw..."

Chapter 3

"I Was At Least Expecting Some Sandwiches"

New Year's Eve had come and gone in a beautiful, chaotic, drunken haze, and as the bright, shiny new year got underway, the haze dissipated. I began to feel like something big was about to happen to us, and with that great sense of anticipation and expectation, the day of the gig came.

Inside me, all the nerves that I had controlled over the festive season began to scratch their way to the surface, making their presence felt. It was the natural exchange for achievement, when you push forward, towards your dreams, I thought, so I soon pushed my worries aside, I was sure that we were ready after all the time we had spent practising, perfecting and polishing our music, surely that would all pay-off, take us through our big day.

In the minute it took me to pull back the metal foil on my favourite chow mein pot noodle at lunchtime and spoon it in, I found my stomach didn't agree with my reasoning, the food-like substance caught in my dry throat. So I chucked the rest of the slimy ringlets in the bin, opting for a cup of tea instead. A while later, with a couple of cups of tea sloshing around in my still unsettled stomach, I left my house and set off for Dave's.

On the afternoon of our biggest gig so far, I took in my surroundings as I paced along. It was clear, fresh and bright, a late rescinding frost drew jewel-like patterns of silver onto the pavement beneath my padding black sixteen-hole D. M's - everything seemed to say, new beginnings, new opportunities, take them while you can – it all starts today.

I vaulted over the churchyard wall into the graveyard, picking up a bit of pace now, feeling revitalized, it really was a beautiful day to be alive. I watched the birds chattering high up on the silent grey stones, smiling at their innocence, the simplicity of their lives, when my old man's New Year's Eve words of wisdom came back to me. 'Hey Mike, watch out for these groupies, they are riddled with gonorrhoea and syphilis'. I snorted trying not to laugh, trying instead to think of my mum's kind smile, the faith she had in me, and her excited call of 'oh good luck, or should I say break a leg?' as I left, but my mind kept filling up with images of inflamed genitals, engorged and weeping. I thought, I know which one of those I'll be thinking about up on stage tonight, laughing to myself, and took a deep breath of the life affirming air, carried on walking down churchyard hill and onto to Dave's house.

I wandered into Ann's kitchen; it was its usual hive of activity; Ann was frying up a huge vat of something that smelled delicious, despite my stomach. Hayley, Jo and Dave's youngest sister, Vicky were all buttering slices of bread on the wooden farmhouse kitchen table at its centre, larking about, while Dustbin the cat looked on, washing a spotless white sock like paw.

Hayley beamed at me, looking particularly pleased with herself. "Hi Skinner, are you ready for tonight?" She asked, her voice full of excitement.

I rubbed my queasy stomach, "Yeah, ready as I'll ever be."

Hayley laughed, "Skinner's here, David!"

Dave came in from the dining room carrying his bass drum case, opened it up. "Check this out- Hayley did it for us," he grinned, revealing a painting of our Virus V1 logo on his bass drum, exactly how it should be, with the jawless skull perched edgily on top of a three-dimensional V.

"Oh what, cheers Hayley, it's brilliant," I said, totally stunned by how good it looked, "Cheers, Hayley," I repeated, feeling a bit lost for words.

I pulled her awkwardly to me and gave her a big hug, she looked a bit taken aback.

"It's alright Skinner, it's fine, you're not going to get all emotional, are you?" She asked, quickly switching her faultless beam back onto her face.

"Well… It's either that or I drop my trousers again," I said, as normal service was resumed.

"No don't do that in the kitchen Skinner, it's very unsanitary," she chided, sending us both into fits of laughter, tightening our hug.

Dave moved in, hands waving like a boxing referee. "OK, break it up, break it up," he said. "I've got Aaron the Ted's phone number, and I'm not afraid to use it!"

"Oh cheers, Dave," I laughed, theatrically dropping her like a hot coal. "Thank you very much," I Elvis-ed.

"OK right, that's better. Let's not see any more of those shenanigans, shall we?" Dave cackled.

I then noticed Dave's bright red hair.

"Is that you as well?" I asked the multitalented Hayley.

She smiled, nodding, giving her handy work the once-over.

"It looks brilliant, you've been busy, haven't you?" I smiled.

Dave laughed, "Yeah, she's like the fifth Virus member."

"She's like the fifth Vi-eatle…" I said, to blank looks, nobody knew what I was on about, so I clarified, "You know like the fifth Beatle… Vi-eatle… No?"

Hayley laughed, "You're a nutter, you are Skinner!"

Alan popped his head around the dining room door. "Is that you, BAKER!?" He enquired, his face creasing up into a smile.

Jo echoed, "BAKER!"

"I heard the word nutter and thought that Baker must be in my house," said Alan, laughing.

"That's a little bit harsh, isn't it?" Dave asked.

I replied, "Harsh realities of life my friend," accordingly.

Alan picked up his teacup and took a sip, "So you've got a gig tonight?"

I nodded steadily grinning back at him.

Alan's face creased up. "Is it by royal appointment then?" He quipped.

Dave sniggered, "I doubt it... We have got a track about the Queen, but she wouldn't like it very much, would she Skin?"

"Nah, nor would the arch bitch of canterbury," I affirmed.

Alan shook his head, "Bloody hell Baker, you don't like authority, do you?"

I nodded. "It's them, they don't like me," I said, almost wisely.

Alan chuckled to himself and repeated, "They don't like me." Setting his teacup down and standing up with purpose,

"I've got some work to do, some of us have still got to scratch out a living!" He laughed, "Good luck for tonight and don't forget me when you're all millionaires."

"Millionaires!!" Dave snorted, "Huh... Pretty unlikely I'd say!"

I laughed, "Cheers Alan!"

Alan grabbed his jacket and made his way to the door, leaving to go price a job up.

Dave and me had a quick brew while chatting with the girls, then we set to work ourselves, loading the gear into the back of the Marina van, being especially careful with our new logoed bass drum – It really looked the business.

*

Once we had loaded up, we said a fond farewell to Ann's kitchen and took the short drive along the A602, and were soon pulling up at the front of Bowes Lyon house in Stevenage. Dave saw a sign that read ARTISTS STAFF V.I.P.S with a red arrow pointing around the back.

"Artists!!! Huh!!!" Dave exclaimed, pulling down hard on the steering wheel.

Dave raised his eyebrows mechanically up and down at me, then followed the red arrow, driving around the narrow pot-holed track to the back of Bowes, where we saw Andy and Whiff waiting, sitting on a low wall. Whiff puffing away steadily on a roll-up, plumes of smoke hiding his face, Andy leaning forwards, looking at the ground, lost in his own thoughts.

"Ah there they are… The artists," Dave grinned, blasting his horn.

"Arse tits more like," I jeered, pulling a Joey Deacon face, giving them both the serial pude pullers sign.

Dave parked up as close as he could to the service entrance, and we both jumped out and began stacking up the gear next to the entrance. Immediately Andy came over, joining us, grabbing a couple of drum cases, while Whiff carried on sitting on the wall, in no hurry to finish his roll-up. It was typical Whiff. He had worked out early on that Dave, Andy and me, to a lesser extent, used to show off who could lift the most gear, but he was never into all that macho type of stuff, so most of the time he would hang back, let the 'hard men' do the work. It had become an inside joke between the three of us, however, Dave wasn't in the mood today, and eyed him as he carefully hoisted the bass drum case onto his shoulder.

"Whiff, come on mate, give us a hand, bloody hell!"

I snorted, "Yeah, bloody hell mate… Have a heart," I Alan-Ed from deep underneath my Laney amp.

Andy grinned mischievously, "Yeah come on, lard arse, move your fat, lardy arse," he said, sending the three of us into hysterics.

Whiff stared at Andy for a moment, smiled wanly, sighed, testily shook his head, then stubbed out his roll-up on his low perch, before marching over to the van. He picked up his amp, chucked it effortlessly up onto his shoulder and walked to the entrance with us, steadily dossing out the back of Andy's turned head.

I walked up to the entrance, gave the grey double doors a gentle knock, fell back a bit, waited.

Dave repeated, "Move your lard arse… That's a little bit harsh, isn't it?"

Dave and me looked to Andy, who answered with the standard, "Harsh realities of life, my friends."

I thumped on the silent door a couple more times, ramping up the force each time.

"I don't think they can hear us; shall we go round the front?" Whiff suggested.

Andy shook his head, "I'm not going around the front... I'm an artiste."

Whiff smirked. "Yeah, a piss artiste," he said, seizing his chance to even things up.

Dave interrupted, "OK ladies, break it up," putting his hands up like a boxing referee.

I aimed a couple of swift kicks at the door, losing my patience, and it flew outwards, revealing a short bloke wearing a Stevenage football club t-shirt.

"Oh... Alright mate, we're Virus V1, we're playing tonight," I said, smiling innocently like I hadn't just tried to kick his door off its hinges.

Stevenage F.C. nodded his head, backed off, indicating that we should follow him, and we went in through a small service area, and out into the main hall.

Whiff spotted the bar to the left of us, cackled, "Is it fucking whisky time Skinner?"

Nah, I've had enough of that now, I thought, "No, it's fucking dickhead time, Whiff." I told him.

Dave and Andy guffawed, pointing at him, and he looked down, went quiet.

In the silent hall, I looked over at the stage- even without any kit on it, it was a lot bigger than I thought it would be. In fact, the whole place looked absolutely massive with no one in the venue. I stopped in front of the stage where only two weeks ago, I had watched Discharge play, the stage that I had seen so many great bands play on since we had discovered Bowes, the stage that we would be playing on in only a few hours' time. I thought, this is going to be amazing, I can't wait to get up there, do it for ourselves, and show people what we can do.

"OK boys, the dressing room's over there, it's just been painted, it should be dry by now, but be careful, I wouldn't put your hands on it," said Stevenage F.C., disturbing me from my reverie, pointing his finger towards the toilets before sloping off in the direction of the bar.

Andy walked ahead of us, went straight past the toilets, which surprised me as I thought they were one and the same thing, but no, we followed him into a clean, brightly coloured dressing room that had a smell of fresh paint and cannabis hanging in the air.

In one corner of the small room, there was a mirror with white bulbs around it, like something out of Broadway show, at the centre, a couple of seats were scattered around a wonky metal table. On the table, there was a crumpled, well-thumbed punk fanzine, with a smiling Beki Bondage on the front, next to it, sat a half empty bottle of water.

"Where's the rider then?" Asked Whiff and the three of us cracked up laughing.

"What were you expecting?" I asked him.

Dave ventured, "Champagne and quail's eggs?"

"A rice pudding?" said Andy smirking.

I snorted, "Whiff mate… You drink the fucking water and
read the fucking magazine, that's the rider," I told him, pointing
at the table.

"I was at least expecting some sandwiches," Whiff
sighed meekly, sending us into fits of laughter all over again.

"Oh, shut up lard boy," Andy mocked.

Whiff snorted, "Oh ha, ha, Andy, give it a rest!"

Andy Judy-ed, "Oh Paul, you can have sandwiches when you come
home… lots of them, van loads of them, truckloads of them, buns,
baps, baguettes, tea cakes"

"OK, Andrew, yeah, yeah," Whiff said impatiently, turning away
from him.

"You've got Beki Bondage, what more do you want, mate?" I said
sitting down, "I'd rider."

Whiff grinned, his eyes passing over Beki's sultry, smiling face on the
cover of the fanzine, over to the bright walls of the dressing room,

"Hmm, I reckon that could do with something, bit plain, isn't it?
...Ta Dah," he said Paul Daniels like, pulling out a permanent
marker pen from his top pocket.

"Oh, nice one Whiff, go for it," I said, cackling.

Whiff shot Dave and me, a mischievous grin, put pen to wall, and
started daubing the Virus V1 logo onto the spotless walls, while the
rest of us stood back to admire his deft, handy work.

On the sixth and possibly most intricate one so far, Stevenage FC
walked in, saw what Whiff was up to, looked like he was going to say
something, then thought better of it, and marched back out of his
not so clean fresh dressing room to the sound of our roaring
laughter. On every wall, there was now a Virus V1 logo, it was
brilliant, with only our daubing's, the dressing room was beginning
to look like a shrine to us, so I grabbed the pen to add my mark
while Andy grabbed his camera, taking a few shots as we posed and
messed about.

A few minutes later while we scribbled away, a group of four blokes
strolled in, one of them was wearing glasses, and I thought, fucking
hell it's Dick the singer with The Subhumans and other guys
from the band. I wanted to stay cool but, I had read in Sounds and
The NME that Dick was a friendly type of bloke who liked a chat, so
I blundered in,

"You alright?" I grinned, catching his eye.

Dick scrutinized me through his thick glasses for what felt like a very
long time, then finally, giving me a cursory nod, he shrugged at the
others, and sat down heavily at the table, picked up the fanzine and

started thumbing through it. Oh what, that's a surprise, I thought they were approachable, talkative … OK, well fair enough, I'm not giving up- I know how to get a conversation going with them- I smoothly slipped my guitar out of my case, plugged it in and let loose with the intro to The Subhumans' track 'Demolition war'.

"You recognise this?" I asked, smiling in their direction.

Dick glanced up from the fanzine, gave me a patient little smile, like he was trying not engage with a particularly annoying little kid and went back to his fanzine. I thought, what a bunch of knobends, they think they're fucking rock stars, you're only humans just like me, no better no worse, what you think you're better than anybody else, just because you've got a record out? Wankers. I dossed them out for a while, shaking my head in their direction as they huddled over the fanzine flipping through its pages, pointing, laughing, making comments, totally ignoring us.

"Phwoar… Look at this," said Dick, salaciously, drooling over a life-sized picture of Beki Bondage's face in the centre page spread.

In a second, all the band grabbed at the fanzine, pulling it this way and that, making noises like Sid James in Carry on Camping and made comments about what they'd like to do to her.

Dick pushed Beki's other suitors aside, announcing to the whole dressing room including us, "I'll show you what I'd like to do to her."

Dick made a hole where her mouth was, smirked towards us, unzipped his trousers, pulled out his worm-like knob and tried to put it through the hole, making the rest of the band bray incessantly. I've fucking had enough of this, I thought, you dirty bastard. I stood up fast, kicked back skidding my chair across the floor into the Virus V1 daubed wall.

"What a bunch of fucking wankers, let's get out of here," I said, loud enough for the fucking wankers to hear.

Andy, Dave and Whiff nodded their approval, followed me out of the now silent dressing room.

In the main hall, away from The Subhumans or The Sadhandjobs, as I was about to christen them, I turned to carry on my rant, and almost bumped into four blokes coming the other way.

I noticed one of them was wearing glasses.

"Err... Skin, I think they're The Subhumans," Whiff said.

"Y...Yeah... Are they? Really?" I said, uncertainly.

Whiff ogled them as they walked past us, nodded, "Yeah, that's definitely them."

"Jesus, thank fuck for that, that bloke, what a prat."

Whiff chuckled, "I know if it makes you feel any better, I thought they were The Subhumans too."

"Bloody hell," I said, slapping my head exasperatedly,

"It was Dick though... Dickhead." I added, quickly recovering,

Whiff laughed, "Yeah, that's about right, what a fucking dickhead."

I thought, well, that was embarrassing, I wonder, will this take over
from 'it's fucking whisky time'? In my all-time fuck up hit parade.
Oh well, it's done now, so trying to forget it, I strolled over
to the stage, where me and Whiff put a couple of roll-ups together to
pass the time.

One of Bowes' sound engineers approached us as Whiff and me sat
puffing away, telling us that it was time for our soundcheck, if we
wanted one, so we dobbed out our roll-ups on the wooden floor, set
up quickly and at his signal, launched into 'V1 Bomb', the track that
had steadily become the bands favourite over time.

I was surprised we didn't sound any different to what we normally
did, then the PA system kicked in and everything changed, our
sound absolutely blasted out into the empty hall. It was heavier,
fuller, but as we carried on through the track, I noticed a couple of
things that could be improved upon, to bring all the different
elements through. Andy's vocals were way too loud, drowning
everyone else out, and although the bass drum was pumping through
good and strong, the rest of the kit was being lost
under the maelstrom of Whiff's bass and my guitar.

A few small alterations were needed, so I made a mental note of
them, and played V1 Bomb through to its end, listening for anything
else that might make our sound better.

"OK?" Asked the sound engineer.

I walked up to Andy's mic, "Yeah, there's a couple of things
mate…"

I heard a click, the hum of The PA system died, and without a backwards glance the sound engineer walked off towards the bar and that was the end of our soundcheck. I thought great, welcome to the world of the support act.

Instead of mooching around the venue or watching wankers be wankers in the dressing room, whilst we waited to go on, we decided to have a look around the town, get a bit of grub and after four fish and chips and a few more roll ups, we wandered back up to Bowes and saw there was a long queue forming outside behind the metal safety barriers. I was surprised with the turn-out, it being so close to New Year's Eve, there were groups of punks, skinheads, rockers and even a few old hippies had ventured out on this cold winter's night, wrapping themselves up warm in their Afghan coats. I was beginning to feel nervous; it didn't last long though, as I had my mates around me and because of that I felt a rush of confidence and my nerves were soon replaced by exhilaration and excitement at the evening in front of us. It was our time to do it.

On the way past the queue, I nodded to a few people, who nodded back uncertainly, with faces that said, who are you? I told myself to calm down a bit, or I could really embarrass myself.

Andy stepped forward at the box office, raising his hand in a wave. "Oh, hi, we are artists, so we don't need to pay," he said, to the decent-looking Siouxsie Sioux clone in the booth.

Siouxsie looked confused, so I gently nudged him aside.

"We're Virus V1, we are playing tonight," I said, sounding more confident than I felt.

Siouxsie smiled, nodded and said 'OK', gesturing for us to go in.

Whiff, Dave, Andy, and me walked in past the public toilets, past the T-shirt sellers and entered the main hall, where we found it was already hot, loud, half full and buzzing with anticipation. Dave at our front leading the way, we wiggled our way through the throngs of people, finally making it to a thankfully now empty dressing room where we sat in silence with our thoughts waiting to be called.

A while later, someone came for us, and we followed them out of the dressing room to wait at the side of the stage while Stevenage F.C., now in a Subhumans T-shirt, introduced us.

"Hello everybody, a Happy New Year to you all, here's our first band of the night, your first band of the year, no pressure lads, by the way...... Give your appreciation to Virus V1!"

Virus V1 walked out onto the massive stage, the blinding lights showing the nervous smiles scrawled onto all of our faces, and we quickly did a few last-minute checks.

Andy drew the mic up, "Whey! Good evening and Happy New Year!"

A couple of cheers came back from the crowd.

"This one's dedicated to all the arse-licking Tories out there; it's called Everybody's Boy!" He announced.

Dave hit the intro, and at the end of the bar, his full kit roll brought us all in perfectly on time and everything clicked. It was incredible, it was lift off, the massive sound vortex of the PA system engulfed the hall, smashing our music and our message into the faces of the audience who responded by jumping, tearing into each other, and seeing the chaos we were creating from up on stage, we reciprocated by throwing everything we had into it.

Whiff was off to my left, his fingers surged, ripping at his bass strings, bending and weaving like he was having a fit. Andy centre stage, was upright, possessed, stalking the stage, a figure of anger and full of energy. Dave, our captain of the beat, laying into the skins and me? I was hammering the chords onto the fretboard, revelling in every fucking second of it. In the middle of Everybody's Boy, when it came to my mini solo -the solo I had fluffed live so many times before, I felt like I couldn't fail, everyone in the venue was willing me to get it right, and as I smoothly went through it, I wondered why I had a problem with it. It was as easy as F, G#, B.

I looked at Dave as my guitar faded away at the end of 'Everybody's boy', the crowd cheering and clapping in its wake, and he beamed back at me, giving me a more than-satisfied nod.

"Cheers, this is for all the people who celebrated Christmas this year, it's called Christ Fuckers," Andy said to the rapidly growing audience.

Dave slammed into the opening beat and once again the audience started bouncing, pushing into each other in anticipation of the raging guitars they knew were about to come.

Andy Chanted, "Symbol of religion, a man in pain, Jesus died well
what a shame, so that we might be forgiven, sin is what you live
in...... You can fuck your own Christ."

Dave lashed into the snare, Whiff and me brought in the raging
guitars, the now sated crowd jumped, clawed, pushed, laughed and
pumped their fists in the air. I was amazed at the sound being
produced by the P.A system, it was incredible; I could feel the air
being forced away from us, our music and our message roaring, like
we were standing behind a 747-jet engine and, right in the firing line
stood the audience. I felt a massive rush of adrenaline course
through me as we all connected in the disorder, up on stage and in
the audience, it was a beautiful kind of chaos, I couldn't
have stopped even if I wanted to, so at the end of 'Christ Fuckers' to
keep the rush going I launched straight into 'Protest', I couldn't help
it.

'Protest' came and went in a savage one-minute thirty-second blur,
the audience showing their approval by clapping, cheering and
stamping their feet on the floor, making the stage shake underneath
us.

On our next number 'Public Enemy' a supposedly slow track, we
started off slowly but as adrenaline pulsed through us all, 'Public
Enemy' soon took on a whole life of its own and began to speed up
with each and every passing verse, I thought we've got to get a grip
here; I got myself under some sort of control, made myself slow up a
bit, playing the track as it should be.

On 'Private War' our next track, my adrenaline came back with a
vengeance. In fact, it took over completely during my intro and I
set the tempo way too fast, and once we had all come in, although it

was hard for us all to keep up, and stay in time, we all rose to the
challenge particularly Dave, whose arms became a blur as he
venomously lashed into the skins. I nervously looked up and around
at everybody, and was relieved to see that not only, did nobody care
about the speed we were playing at, the audience were lapping it up
too.

'S.S.P.G' came next, a medium-paced number about the notorious
Special Patrol Group, the Tories answer to low-level inner-city
crime, who were basically a bunch of bullies with badges,
and the knowledgeable crowd reacted by singing the chorus of
'S.S.P.G' back to us, cheering and clapping as it faded at the end.

Intro duties were back on me for our next track, the ultra-fast 'No
More Genocide', and thankfully, this time I kept my rushing
adrenaline under control, setting the right tempo. It was a good thing
too, as Dave was at full capacity on that one, and after my intro, he
hit the drum roll bringing Whiff and Andy in, and we watched
the floor explode in front of us again, as our sound
blitzed the audience squeezing out the silence, filling every part
of the hall.

In front of Whiff, there were a group of goth and punk girls
at the front of the stage, and when he did his solo bars
after the second chorus, some of them pointed screaming
lecherously at him. I thought you lucky bastard, then, my old man's
cautionary words came back to me about the dangers of groupies,
the gonorrhoea, the syphilis, and before I knew it, my mind filled
with images of the weeping sores and pus-filled buboes. I pushed my
guitar hard into my groin in anticipation of the inevitable umbrella
treatment that would follow such dangerous liaisons, then I laughed
to myself and thought, you really have got to stop listening to him.

'Suffer Little Children' followed: I hit the intro, sending the place
into bedlam again, Dave and me exchanged a grin as we saw our first
crowd surfer being passed jauntily from shoulder to shoulder. I
nodded at Dave thinking, groupies, crowd surfers, yep, we've made it
now, and we both creased up, as he was unceremoniously dropped
to the floor, only to re-appear at the front of the stage with a big
smile on his face. Andy was enjoying himself too as he passed the
mic out into the crowd and his mates bellowed
'Suffer Little Children' on the chorus back at us.

'Horrors of Belsen' was up next, we hadn't played it live before, so I
felt a bit nervy when Whiff began to pluck out the intro. I need not
have worried as 'Horrors of Belsen' with its sound of creeping death
went down well with the Bowes audience, it encapsulated them in a
way that was almost hypnotic. I watched as their heads slowly
nodded, their eyes telling me that they were miles away, and I
thought that not only our music was hitting home, our message is
too.

Intro duties were on me again on our second new live track
'Auschwitz 84' with a single note on the guitar, which undulates and
builds, waiting for Whiff to come in. It undulated and built, built and
undulated, undulated, built. I thought, where the fucking hell
is Whiff, he should be coming in by now, only to glance over to his
side of the stage and there he was, exchanging air kisses with his little
Siouxsie harem in the front row. I couldn't help but laugh, that is
until my bollocks cramped up, as the thoughts of steel umbrellas and
penicillin filled my mind once again.

Dave chucked a spare stick at him, bringing him back into the band,
Whiff laughed, giving him a sarcastic little wave and smiled self-

consciously. I hit the intro again and this time he came in on time, followed by Dave, then Andy, and we were off. Once again, the sound from the towering P.A. system before us pulverized the audience and although everybody's energy levels were beginning to wane, people were still smiling, laughing and throwing what was left of their drinks in the air, some catching the splashes of precious juice in their parched mouths.

In front of us, a sea of faces, crazy people with happy faces, enjoying the moment. I wanted to stay on stage all night and just keep on playing, but 'V1 Bomb' was our last track, our best track, the track we wanted people to think about, hopefully, long after we had left the stage, so if we couldn't carry on, and play an encore, then I was going to put everything I had left into this one, and looking at my mates, Andy, Dave, and Whiff, I could see they were thinking exactly the same thing I was- we steeled ourselves for one last massive sonic attack.

Dave hit the military snare roll, two bars in, I hit the dampened guitar riff, Dave did the full kit roll, and we all came in blitzing the audience, and they responded in kind, finding more energy from somewhere, they jumped, pogoed, slamming into each other and on the chorus grabbing at Andy's mic hungrily and shouted 'V1 bomb' back to us. It was beautiful, it was pure, it was mayhem, it was chaotic, and when the track came to its raucous end two minutes thirty later, we strolled confidently off the stage to a mass of cheers and applause. I thought this is amazing, all of our hard work really is going to pay off after all, now that we are playing to our people. People who liked what we liked, bought the same stuff we did, people who felt strongly about the world and society as a whole. It was simple: we got them, they got us, and together we are going to make a huge angry, energy-filled statement, that we are not like them.

The Tories, The Reds, The Liberals and all their sycophantic cronies working within the government, we are going to tell them. We won't live like you, we are different, we want to live the lives that we choose, NOT YOU - If they don't like it then 'FUCK THE STATE, WE DON'T NEED IT'.

Whiff nudged me as we entered the dressing room, "You alright, Skin?"
"Earth calling Skinner, earth calling Skinner, come in, Skinner!" A sweat drenched grinning Dave asked.

I smiled wanly back at them, sat down heavily on the chair, totally drained, "Yeah sorry about that, I was tripping out."

I examined my glistening face in the lighted mirror and thought Jesus, that really was hard work-I'll have to tell the old man that, not that he would believe it though, recently he had been pulling my leg about that Dire Straits song 'Money for nothing', the one about getting a little blister on my finger or thumb, if only he knew. I smiled, shook my head, he would never know.

Whiff sat down next to me at the lowly table and drunk the half bottle of water down in one, "Aaaahhh that's better."

"See the rider's not so bad, is it?" I laughed.

Whiff grinned, wiping at his parched lips, "I don't know where this is going... Or how long it's going to go on for, all I know is I want to get a record out, that's all I want."

Andy Dave and me all nodded our heads in agreement.

"Yeah, an album, that would be good," I said, thoughtfully.

Whiff stood up with a renewed purpose, "I'll drink to that, who fancies a drink then?"

"Yeah," said Dave, wiping his brow.

Andy said "OK," stretching his arms.

"I'm up for that" I said, sliding my guitar safely away into its case.

No more to discuss, we decamped to the bar and settled back with a couple of pints of snakebite to watch the real Dick and The Subhumans.

Chapter 4

'Bonny and Clyde? Nah, More Like Joey and Jolea Deacon'

A couple of weeks went by, and we were all still buzzing about the
Bowes Lyon House gig. It wasn't like we thought we'd made it or
anything as conventional as that. We just thought that we had moved
up a notch, furthered our cause, and were ready to be a proper
support band – maybe go on tour with one of the signed bands.
Whiff and Andy had steadily been putting out feelers around Ware
and Hertfordshire, while I was keen to talk to Dave about him
getting a double bass drum kit, to not only give our music a heavier
sound, but to have something different from all the other second
and third wave punk bands that were coming up. Dave was a
massive Motorhead fan and when we had talked about it in the past.
He had laughed, saying he could be the 'Philthy Animal' Williams of
Virus V1 with a twin bass kit. I laughed at the time too, but the more
I thought about it, a political punk band with walls of Discharge
guitars and a twin bass drum kit at its centre was very appealing. It
would leave heads ringing for days.

I went round for Dave to see what he had to say, and found
Hayley alone in the kitchen, at the sink, washing up after dinner, and
asked her where he was.

"Oh, hi Skinner, he's seeing Steph, again," she replied, raising her
eyebrows.

"Is everything alright with those two?" I asked, catching her look.

"I don't know, he hasn't said anything to me, has he said anything to you?" She asked, dousing a baking tray into the foamy water.

I shook my head, "No."

Hayley turned, looking me directly in the eye, "Something's not right though, Skinner?"

"No, it isn't."

Hayley's eyes bore into me, hoping for an answer. "Hmm, he's irritable, not Dave like at all, he's not being himself," she said searchingly.

I knew what Steph could be like, it wasn't anything new, it was common knowledge, I remembered what Cerys had said about it when Taddy had gone out with her - the possessiveness, the jealousy, the controlling - it could be bringing him down, I didn't know. One thing I did know was, Hayley was lovely, even standing at the sink, dressed in Ann's pinny with her hands covered in soap suds, she looked incredible. I took her in for a while, her red lips, her now spiked up blonde hair, her oh shit, I suddenly realised I was standing in a room alone with Hayley, her deep green eyes sifting through my mind, reading my thoughts.

"Er… I think I'd better go now," I said quickly.

"OK Skinner, yes you can go now," she replied, sniggering at my sudden awkwardness.

I raised my hand in a little wave, "See ya!"

"Yeah, see ya, Skinner."

I swallowed deeply, nodded like I had been excused, and left
for the pub, thinking it over on the way, and to tell the truth, I
wasn't really worried about Dave. He knew what was what, especially
when it came to girls, as he lived in a house full of them, he always
seemed relaxed around them, but he just hadn't been his usual easy-
going self recently. Whiff had made a couple of jokes at his expense
at our last practice, and instead of laughing them off or turning them
around, giving it back to him like he usually did, he had looked
pissed off.

On the way back up the hill after the practice, with just the two of us
sitting in his van, pitching and rocking over the potholes of the dust
track, he had told me in no uncertain terms, "That Whiff had better
watch his mouth, or there's going to trouble."

I snorted doubtfully, remembering Whiff's throw away comment
about him 'thinking he was a big M, a big M.A.N' like on the Crass
track, when he was heaving some gear into the pavilion.

"Oh, he's only messing around, you know what he's like, we've had
this before, remember?"

Dave shook his head, "I know what he's like, but I'm not taking any
crap from him, Skin."

Whiff could take things too far sometimes; I had seen him do it to
Andy on numerous occasions. Andy was a bit younger than us
though, it was like water off a duck's back to him, mostly, he would
just grin and bear it. It sounded like Dave wasn't going to - not this
time.

"Dave, mate, don't worry about it, I'll have a word with him, it was fine last time, wasn't it?"

"Yeah, I know he's a good bloke, really… A good laugh and all that, but sometimes though…," he trailed off, sniffed hard, turning his nose up.

I nodded, fully understanding. I thought it was hilarious when Whiff was doing it to someone else, someone outside the band, it could be funny with Andy too sometimes, but Dave and me had boundaries, lines we wouldn't cross, even with our mates.

"OK, it's fine, Dave, leave it with me, I'll have a word, he listens to me, well sometimes." I laughed.

In The Tap later that week, at the beginning of another session on the snakebites, I told Whiff that he had gone too far with Dave, to leave it out and at first, typical Whiff, he thought I was joking, tried to laugh it off. It was no joke I assured him I was serious, Dave was pissed off with him, he still tried to laugh it off, but that was the end of it, he went easier on Dave after that.

International diplomat and Nobel peace winner Henry Kissinger could do with a couple of snakebites after averting another potential band crisis, I thought, and, right on cue, as my ruminative walk ended, there I was, opening the door and walking into The Anchor.

Immediately, I felt the warmth radiating from the pubs open fireplace. It crackled, welcomingly in the corner where the older pub veterans congregated to keep the mid-winter's cold at bay, while playing dominoes, telling their tales of woe, and generally getting shitfaced.

Steph and Dave sat in one of the snugs in the main bar
by the window, the orange of the street lights outside blazing in on them, lighting them up like Broadway. I was about to go over and say hello when I noticed Steph gesticulating wildly with her hands, having her say about something or other. Dave was slumped forward on his seat listening, eyes big like saucers, nodding slowly at the assault. It didn't look like a good time to me, so instead I called out and waved.

Dave smiled, waved back happily, while Steph gave me a foreboding 'stay-away-from-us' rictus smile. A warning I took heed of, going straight to the bar, ordered a nice, refreshing pint of snakebite from Stewart, who eyed me accusingly, still angry with everyone about the destruction of his nativity scene. I thought you know nothing mate, I was well hidden away in the Marina.

A cheer went up in our part of the pub, as I waited for the miserable barman to pour my pint, and I thought, oh well at least someone was having a good time in The Anchor tonight. I looked in
through the internal window and saw there was a rowdy darts game in progress.

Stewart thumped my pint down in front of me, bringing me back from my thoughts, he snatched my last fiver from my steady hand, chucked it into the cash register, returning with a meagre amount of change, which I put into my pocket with the other coins.

"Cheers, Skinner," he spat.

"Yeah, cheers Stewart," I spat back, left the grumpy twat to his grumpy twatiness and walked into our part of the pub, the life and soul of the place tonight, see who was in.

Craig, Taddy, Ronnie, Dale Murphy, Coop's, Mal, Robin 'Robber' Banks, Dave 'Satellite Ear's Negus, Tom 'Thumb' Neville, and Lee and Glyn surrounded the dartboard, most of their girlfriends, sitting back, drinking, chatting, smoking, watching the game.

In amongst the girls sat Phil chatting with his older sister, Clare, who I was surprised to see out and about as her stepdad had pretty much put her on a leash since she had become a teenager. Clare was a couple of years older than me- really good-looking, in fact, she was even more beautiful than the last time I had seen her, three years earlier - I went to say hello.

"I haven't seen you for a while, have you been let out?" I asked, breaking up their conference.

Phil looked up, laughed "Yeah, she's escaped Skinner,"

"Why do you want to hang around with village yobbos, they're no good, get it right, Buckfield." he intoned, going into his well-known impression of his stepdad.

I placed my pint on their table, sat down in between them, "He's right though, the village is full of yobbos," I said nodding towards Craig and Taddy at the dart board.

Clare laughed in that easy, carefree way I remembered from the other fleeting times we had shared together when we were younger, before her incarceration.

I took Clare in, "You look nice, you must be going on somewhere afterwards?" I asked, cheekily, seeing she was well over-dressed for a midweek night at The Anchor in her black suit jacket, tight white shirt and black mini skirt.

"Aw thanks Skinner. No, I've been to a job interview in Ware," she chuckled, taking a sip of her drink.

"Oh yeah what was it for?"

"A Trainee Accountant."

"Yeah, and I bet you got it too!"

Clare laughed, "Oh, thanks, yeah, I should do, my friend's dad owns the company, I've sort of jumped the gun… I came straight here to celebrate." she said, taking another sip of her drink. "And to escape the stepdad too, the pillock" she smirked, rolling her eyes dramatically.

Phil cracked a smile and went into another one of his impersonations, "Why hang around with the yobbos, Clare? Do something with your life: You should get it right, Buckfield."

I shook my head, mystified, "Why does he call you Buckfield, when your name's Buttercroft?"

Phil replied, "I don't know, he always has done."

I snorted, "No offence, but your stepdad sounds like a right wanker."

"He is!" Both of them answered in unison.

Phil said, "Oops... Jinx," and they touched pinky fingers to keep the Buttercroft gremlin at bay.

In time, it became Phil's turn at the oche, so he went off to play darts with the lads, leaving Clare and me to catch up – we had a lot of catching up to do.

Clare had moved into the village around the time I had gone to Richard hole school, with her mum being single at the time, she was free to come and go as she pleased and hung out in the village with the rest of us, having a laugh, getting up to mischief.

Once her mum had remarried 'The Keyholder' or 'The Pillock' as Clare called him, she was a rare sight around the village, and I suddenly realised how much I missed her. In fact, human nature being what it is, now she wasn't available, was out circulation, I wanted her even more. I had a massive crush on her and as we talked tonight, I started to remember why, as not only was she beautiful and stylish, she was also funny and intelligent too.

Clare and me chatted away like The Key holder had never come between us. It was hard to believe, after all this time, she was just like the girl I used to hang out with outside the local village shop, secretly eating the chocolate bars and chewing gum we had just nicked, and as the snakebites and vodka and oranges came and went, we opened up about our lives, talked candidly, and inevitably we got closer, and our connection strengthened. I loved the way she talked about her 'pillock of a stepdad', he really was her jailer, she wasn't having any of it though, she would run rings around him, she would climb out of her bedroom window after The Pillock and her mum had gone to bed, see her mates in Ware, then in the early morning as the sun came up, she would drunkenly climb back into her window and no one would be any the wiser.

One day she told me, he had spotted her in the back garden in the early hours, coming back after a proper session, marched out to remonstrate with her and she had told him that it was such a nice morning she had got up early to walk the family dog and he had believed her. I couldn't believe it, he had actually believed her, despite the fact that she was in a mini skirt and Frank the family dog had been curled up asleep in his basket, in front of their aga.

I cracked up laughing, "What a pillock," I said draining another pint of congealed nectar.

"Pillock by name, Pillock by nature," she assured me, chucking back another V&O.

I cackled at her wisdom, "I don't know, maybe it's a parent thing, I've got a few stories about my old man too, he can be really weird too."

"Mmmm can he out pillock, The Pillock though?" she said grabbing her refill.

I took a long draft of my refill, and told her about some of my old man's idiosyncrasies, the way he, a highly paid executive, would go to a jumble sale, buy a decent worn pair of shoes for ten pence, even though they were way too small for him, then hobble around like a traditional Chinese girl with tiny golden lotus feet. I told her about the way he would argue incessantly with the T.V, a box of lights,

74

which sat in the corner of the room, which of course never answered back and funniest of all. I told her about what my mum called his izums, my old man's izums changed constantly, it could be anything from Yogurt eaters to hitch hikers, to bell ringers to bee keepers, he would pick someone out in society, someone who was slightly different, and blame them for all of society's ills, it was ridiculous, it was lunacy, it was fucking hilarious.

In the hour between ten o'clock and last orders at eleven o'clock, I put my hand into my pocket, digging deep, and I found that my meagre cash reserves had almost run dry.

"What's the matter?" Clare asked, seeing my face clouding over.

"I'm sorry I'm skint. I've only got enough for one more round," I sighed. "For us," I added, shiftily looking around.

She waved it away, "Oh, don't worry about it, it's fine, I'm celebrating, anyway I'll be rich soon."

"OK, but the next time I see you I'll..." I stopped myself, gave her a what am-I-talking-about look and we both dissolved into laughter.

I went to the serving hatch, ordered from the still seething Stewart, and he stalked off, returning a few minutes later with a frothing pint of snakebite and a tangy vodka and orange.

"Two pound ninety," he demanded.

 I snorted, placed my meagre stash of coins into his open hands, and he impatiently counted them out.

"One, two, three, fifty pence coins, one, two ten pence coins and a oh a bunch of brass," he said fingering the coins, like he was looking for fakes.

Once satisfied they were all legal tender, he
said, "Cheers, Skinner." Putting the brass aside, "I'll put that into the collection box for next year's Christmas decorations, shall I?"

I creased up remembering Phil the Grinch's calamitous cartoon car park driving on New Year's Eve, on the night we got away in a Marina, then I saw the hawk-like look on Stewart's face and reigned it in, it was too late though. Stewart pulled a crocodile smile, nodded knowingly to himself, now he knew for sure that his suspicions were, indeed - correct. I was one of his nativity-scene-wreckers and he dossed me out menacingly, all the way back to my seat.

Clare asked, "What was all that about?" Glaring back at the fuming Stewart.

"Oh, it was Phil, he crashed into Stewpot's nativity scene in Dave's van on New Year's Eve, rammed Rudolf, gave him a red nose, decapitated an innocent Christmas tree too, dragged it down Anchor Lane under the van, I thought he would have told you that?"

Clare creased up laughing. "Oh my god, no he didn't, I can believe it though he was in a right state when he got in that night," she said, moving a manicured hand onto my leg, giving it a playful squeeze, "What's it got to do with you though, if he was driving?"

"I don't know, I was his co-pilot, maybe he thinks I was driving," I replied, gently squeezing her hand. "Seriously, he drove home… I cannot believe he actually got that far; he was totally wasted out of his tree, out of his Christmas tree, should I say," I said, smiling lopsidedly.

"No, he was fine," Clare quipped, grinning from ear to ear.

"Oh what, so he did tell you?"

"Not about the Christmas trees, he didn't, but he told me he was 'fine to drive' after he had left the van parked up on the front lawn back at our house, kept on saying it over and over again."

"On the lawn?"

"Yep, on the lawn, the Keyholder went epileptic in the morning, 'Oh no what have you done to my lovely lawn, I've just put weed and feed on it, you must have been drinking and driving Buckfield'."

I creased up, "Nah, he was fine, fine."

Clare convulsed with laughter, drained her drink and banged the empty glass onto the table, "I need to get fine, what about you?"

"Cheers, go on then," I said, looking at my half-empty pint and she decamped for the serving hatch.

A couple of minutes later Clare reappeared through the mass of teenagers crowded into our bar, balancing two snakebites, two vodka and oranges and two packets of crisps on a tray, then mission completed, she set it down, and said, "I thought it might save some time."

I nodded at her ingenuity, we were clearly on a mission now, so we linked up like drunks in arms, and got stuck in throwing them back.

In the background, as the darts game got louder and louder, so we could hear each other, we got closer and closer until we were nose-to-nose, looking deep into each other's eyes. I could feel her warm breath on me, I thought if I move forward one inch, I will be kissing your sweet, cherry-red lips, I couldn't stop myself, so I moved forward, our lips met.

"Oi," I heard from behind, pulled back from the cherries to see Taddy's grinning face gawking at me, Craig standing next to him grinning wagging his finger.

"None of that in here," he said. "It's a family pub."

I chuckled, gave him the all too familiar two-fingered salute, and he creased up, and they turned back to their game of darts.

Clare and me moved back in on each other again, I heard another shout and I thought, oh yeah, once is funny, twice you can fuck off mate. I swung around; it was Dave.

I stood up, "Whey Dave! How's it going man?" Shaking his hand.

Dave smiled, "I've had better nights, sorry about Steph earlier on, mate."

"Oh what? Don't worry about it, mate, it wasn't you, was it?" I said evenly.

He looked down, mumbled, "Well, at least someone thinks that it wasn't me."

"I'm not to blame for everything…" he continued, trailing off.

"What happened?"

"Ah, nothing, everything, I don't know really, I'll tell you about it later, look, she's gone home now… So, since my night's basically over, I'm off too."

Dave looked over to Phil, who was standing next to the still grinning Taddy and Craig, "You need a lift mate? I can take you back if you like."

Phil looked over to his sister, to see if she wanted a lift too, and my head almost flopped onto the table. Oh no, please not now, I thought please, mate, do fuck off, we're having the time of our lives here, if she goes now, that will be it, I might never see her again.

"What? Oh no, no, I'm not going anywhere, I'll get a taxi back later. Tell the silly toss pot I'm having a few drinks with my new work colleagues," she said, chasing away my blues, keeping my head upright and off the fucking table.

Phil laughed over his shoulder. "OK sis, I'll tell the silly toss pot just that, you know what, he'll probably believe it too," he said as him and Dave left us.

I felt a little ray of sunlight shine on me as they left our rowdy little bar, saying their goodbyes, and now with her little brother gone. It wasn't long before Clare's arms sort out my torso, pulling me in close. She smiled serenely at me as she rested her head on my shoulder, the two of us cozying back up again, sitting knee to knee, watching the darts, a game that had gotten louder by the minute, so much so that Stewart marched in, asked them to keep it down a bit.

Craig came over as the more informed, even more pissed off Stewart departed, generously bringing us a couple of drinks and asked us if we wanted to have a game of doubles with him and Taddy, who we knew had been winning all night. Craig and Taddy were so full of confidence that I thought it's only them that had anything to lose-we are just drunks in arms.

In one go, Clare downed her voddy, wiped her lips and we strolled over, taking our position at the oche; I had been using pubs since I was fifteen, so I had played plenty of darts over the years. I soon found out that Clare had played a bit too and much to their discomfort, and everyone else's enjoyment 'the Invincibles' were beaten as they struggled in the mad house of double one. Clare and me left the oche to gleeful cheers and a round of applause from their watching girlfriends, some of the others they had beaten that night brought us drinks too and we retired unbeaten to our seats, knocked them straight back.

On the stroke of eleven, Stewart, who despite all the money being made, was still as happy as a yuppy at a GBH gig, rang the bell for last orders. So, we grabbed one more each, downed them, said goodbye to everyone, and stumbled out of the warm pub, into the icy cold air of the night.

Immediately my head cleared outside of the hot stuffy pub, I took a deep breath, filling my lungs and held it down greedily like it was my first cigarette of the day, it was invigorating life affirming, I felt indestructible. I took a step forward and my foot slipped hazardously.

"Whooaaa," I said looking down.

"Whooo," Clare agreed.

On the pavement beneath us, a frost had taken hold, gossamer-thin webs spun out in every direction, glinting up at us under the orange glow of the street lights.

I felt Clare's hand searching for mine, I quickly took it, feeling its warmth, grinned at her, and we unsteadily walked up towards the taxi rank in front of The Feathers Inn.

Clare lunged forwards, slipping on the icy webs, I grabbed her elbow, steadying her.

"I'm fine, fine," she cackled, maniacally.

"Yeah, you are… You're more than fine!" I said, pulling her gently towards me.

Clare's eyes twinkled back at me, under the jewelled sky, "Aw, cheers Skinner, that's cute!"

"Come one, let's get you across this road in one piece, shall we, young lady?" I said, masterfully putting one arm around her waist, the other on her shoulder, just to make sure.

Clare and me tentatively crossed the road, giggling at our immobility, and then as we reached the pavement on the other side, my foot flipped out losing purchase on the treacherous diamond like surface.

I thought I was going over, braced myself for the fall, then her arms pulled back me up, coming to my rescue.

"Skinner, you're not drunk, by any chance, are you?" Asked Clare, grinning.

I cracked up, "I'm off my dial Clare, well either that or I've Joey Deacon's legs bolted on, what about you?"

"Truth be told, I am totally shit-faced."

"Oh what, look, we're not so bad, we made it across the road, didn't we?" I stated inconclusively, as my other foot skidded off the pavements edge.

"Easy now Joey," said Clare, spinning me around in the direction of the taxi rank.

"Oi, oi, watch it, if I'm Joey Deacon, you must be Jolea Deacon," I said, dissolving into fits of laughter, swaying haphazardly like a sapling in a Cornish wind.

"No way I'm the interpreter bloke, what is his name, Ernie?"

"Ernie, yeah that's him, Joey would say, Errrrrrhhgh, Uuuuugghh and Ernie would say 'he said, The Pythagorean Theorem states that for any right triangle, the sum of the squares of the lengths of the legs is always equal to the square of the length of the hypotenuse'."

Clare giggled, "Ernie just made it up as he went along, I thought that."

"Winging it, fucking winging, he was," I laughed, "Clever bloke that Ernie, I liked him better when he was with Bert though."

"What? What are you going on about, Skinner? You're rambling."

"No, no, no, I'm not, he was on Sesame Street, with Bert, you know Bert and Ernie."

Clare snorted, "Oh yeah, he looks different though, amazing what a bit of slap can do."

"Yeah… It is, it mended his legs too," I quipped as we came up to the taxi rank.

"We made it," said Clare, both of us smiling at our over-achievement.

"Cheers Clare, I don't think I would have made it without you."

Clare laughed her sweet laugh again, looked penetratingly into my eyes, "Anytime Skinner."

You are so lovely, I thought, I've just got to kiss you right now.

"Come here," I said, pulling her gently towards me.

Clare came to me easily, I kissed her full on the lips, she opened her mouth, pushed her tongue into my mouth, seeking out my tongue. I pulled her closer, and as I did a beautiful sensation rushed through me, our tongues entwined probing inside our willing mouths, our warm hands on each other's bodies, exploring. I breathed her in, she smelled of cigarettes and alcohol.

Clare pulled back, "I want to go somewhere quiet, just the two of us, let's go somewhere," she whispered in my ear, sending tingles down my spine.

"OK, yeah, come on then," I replied, trying to sound cool.

"Let's go back to yours, I want you now."

"Nah… We can't, we'd never get past my old man; he never goes to bed before I do, he says he likes to put the house to bed himself," I said, shaking my head sadly.

I exhaled an icy plume, thinking, thinking, thinking. It's way too cold out here for a walk out into the fields, so that's out, under the bridge, nope, same problem, and we'd probably fall into the river rib, catch fucking hypothermia, maybe sneak back into The Anchor, go into the bogs, nope Stewart never cleans the bogs, it's foul in there, there's still puke on the floor from The Christmas holidays, anyway he's already pissed off with me. I could be barred, I couldn't live without The Anchor, so no fucking way, hold on.

"I've got an idea, follow me," I said, having a eureka moment, like the wanker in the bath.

She giggled, grabbing my hand, "Ooooh where are we going? This is exciting, isn't it?"

"See that house back there, it's been done up, it's empty, there's no one home, let's check it out."

"OK Skinner, good idea, lead the way… you're mad you are."

Clare and me stumbled back down the road, helping each other along, giggling like little kids, carefully trying to stay up right until we got to the beginning of the terraced houses at the bottom of The Feathers expansive beer garden. I checked to see if there was anyone about, I couldn't believe my eyes, back down the road Ski Sunday, Coop's, and Mal were pacing off in the opposite direction with similar things on their minds, totally unaware of our presence. So we silently slunk off down the path that led around the back of the properties to the empty house, and we found that away from the orange glare of the street lights, it was completely dark. A few tentative blind steps, and we found the pathway to the empty house - nothing was going to stop us now, we were burning hot, our hands finding any excuse to touch each other.

A few bedroom lights shone out like lone beacons above us, thankfully, it was all quiet, the coast was clear, so carefully, minding the builders' materials stacked up around the garden path and various other detritus, we hesitantly walked up into a small porch at the back of the property. On the doorstep, I could just about make out an upturned flowerpot in the gloom, Clare saw it too, lurched forward, and swept it over with her hand in the hope there might be a key. No chance.

I thought it's going to take a bit more ingenuity than that to get us in- I didn't have any ingenuity, however, I did have a pair of sixteen-hole D.M.s, though, so I gave the dilapidated old door a decent sold kick- it cracked, rattled, gave a bit.

"Shhhhh!" Clare said, in an exaggerated tone, giggling.

I shushed her back, grimacing, took aim again.

"Open Sesame, Street," I said, giving it a proper booting, sending it splintering, inwards.

Clare and me peered in.

Inside, there was an almost-empty kitchen, the place had been gutted: a white butler sink, the only remaining feature glowed ghost-like back at us from under the filthy sash window.

"I love this, it's like we are Bonnie and Clyde, Skinner," said Clare, her eyes twinkling mischievously at me. "Bonnie and Clyde lived a life together and finally together they died," she sang tunefully.

"I thought we were Joey and Jolea Deacon."

Clare gave me a playful nudge from behind sending me forward, and we blundered into the darkness of the kitchen, holding our arms out in front of ourselves like we were blind, crashing into stuff, laughing as we went. In front of us, at the end of the kitchen, there was a glimmer of orange light piecing through the gaps of a door frame, so I headed towards the light, fumbled for the doorknob, found it, twisted it, opening the door with a spooky creak, and we found ourselves looking into the front room.

I wandered into the orange glow in the front room, Clare following close behind, the happy couple, home hunters, perusing the Deacon's new family abode, for the next ten minutes or so anyway. It was perfect, still carpeted and in front of us lay a net curtained bay window opening to the street, which let in the warm orange glow from the street lights outside.

"How's this then?" I smiled, turning to Clare.

Clare didn't hang about, she answered me in kind, coming to me quickly, kissing me eagerly on the lips. Immediately we were all over each other, lost in the moment, exploring each other's bodies, we undressed carelessly without regard, throwing our clothes onto the carpeted floor.

Once we had undressed, I watched, mesmerized as she lay down underneath the bay window in the orange glow of the street lights, the shadow of the window frame forming a beautiful arc across her smooth, buttercream-white body. I thought she looked translucent, like a vision, a beautiful celestial body waiting for me. It was just the two of us now, I slowly moved to get on top of her, hesitated, taking her in.

"Oh, don't worry Skinner. I'm on the pill," she whispered

I thought nothing could have been further from my mind… I just wanted to imprint this image onto my memory forever.

Clare smiled, gently coaxed me down onto her, gasping as I entered her. She was wet, wet but tight, she gripped me hard, began to rock, locking her imploring lips onto mine, I pushed my tongue into her mouth, wanting to taste her, taste all of her.

I thrust forwards and backwards, Clare responded by bucking her hips, moaning softly into my ear, building up in volume and in a moment, all the alcohol induced drowsiness had drained from me, all the cold of the night vanished. It felt good. It felt right. We were on top of the world, lost in an amazing feeling of love, hope, desire, and ecstasy.

Clare uncoupled her mouth from mine, decamping to my neck, using her teeth, nibbling, using her tongue, licking, using her mouth to suck, tease, tantalize, stimulating, sending shivers down my spine while I pulled her legs up higher and higher to penetrate deeper and deeper inside her. Clare and me stayed locked as one in joint ecstasy, coming together under the orange vortex of the street lights, two celestial bodies joined together completed, their journey over now.

In the moments afterwards we lay spent, entwined in each other's arms until the cold air eventually drove us back into our clothes, and then the reality of the situation we in, what we had done, returned with a vengeance, there was a real possibility of frostbite, there was real possibility of being caught. We had to get out, but we were as pissed as a couple of judges.

On the way-out, back in the kitchen, back in the darkness once again, I felt her hands on me. Clare engulfed me in her arms, and we shared a long warming embrace, then we dodged back out of the house into the even colder night air, and as I closed the door behind us, it felt like I was not only closing the door of the house, but to the whole experience with Clare too.

On the path out of the Deacon household Clare and me passed under the oblivious bedroom lights, with their oblivious occupants, and it was like something had switched off in the Deacon family, I think we both knew that Joey and Jolea would never work, and whatever tonight was, it wasn't the basis for any kind of relationship, as we lived in two completely different worlds - Two worlds that had collided so beautifully and concisely but ultimately are incompatible, those worlds must eventually go back to their original orbits, or they will wilt and die.

Once we arrived at the taxi rank, we talked about 'our'
house, the darts match, the good night we had shared together, how
drunk we were, I even told her of the beautiful arc, everything,
anything, apart from us and what would happen next as we
knew there would be no next. It was only a one-night stand, but
what a stand, it was a grandstand. I couldn't help feeling a bit sad
when her taxi eventually arrived, and we shared one final long kiss
goodnight, and she was gone, her taxi's tail lights, slowly going up
High Cross Hill and then blinking out at the top.

I sighed, a roll-up seemed like a good idea, so with cold shaking
hands, I deftly put one together before setting off for home. Once
made, I sparked it up, inhaled deeply, feeling exhilarated, feeling the
nicotine, feeling light-headed, I couldn't stop grinning to myself.

In the early hours of the morning, I strolled up along the now silent
A10 puffing away, blowing out huge plumes of smoke and frosty air,
up past the Deacon's old residence, past The Anchor and up onto
the bridge, then something made me stop. I looked over the edge,
away from the street lights and there in the deep watery depths, the
last two of the still working traffic lights Dave and me had chucked
in flashed back at me. I watched for a while, enchanted by them, it
was the same warm orange glow that I had seen back at the house
with Clare.

I thought, two lights pulsing in harmony, life is good, and it really
was.

Chapter 5

Danny Just Loves It When a Plan Comes Together

I woke up late the next morning, and even though I felt groggy, and
my stomach was complaining, the world was good with me. A few
weeks ago, we had played our biggest gig so far, and last night I had
got pissed up, broken into a house and had sex with one of the best-
looking girls in the village. I smiled at the memory of Clare lying
beneath me in the orange glow of the street lights, shook my head
still not quite believing it and then, believing it. I chuckled to myself,
slung my feet out of my warm bed, grabbed my bondage trousers,
hoisted them up, and went downstairs to get a bit of grub to ease my
sloshy stomach.

Once I had filled up on tea, toast and half a Pot Noodle from the
night before, chatting away with the old man and mum, who were
having their lunch. I slouched back up to my room to get back to
some tracks I was working on. It had been a productive time for me
after Bowes. I had written three new tracks in the last week alone.
'Let your slaves go', about the apartheid system in South
Africa, 'Pathetic' about Margaret Thatcher's Y.O.P. scheme, which
was about cheap labour and the exploitation of youth, and a blinder
called 'IRA Ireland' about the troubles in Northern Ireland. I was
particularly pleased with the lyrics on that one, 'Bobby Sands died
for nothing, like so many others, as so-called Christians, kill their so-
called brothers'.

On top of those three stormers, I had written a whole batch of new
guitar riffs, varying from nasty slow grinders to ultra-fast thrash
tracks, which I could remember even without consulting my tracks
book – always a sign of good quality. It was time to do something

with them, to keep the band moving forward. In the weeks leading up to Christmas, I had a spell of lyric writing; politics, religion, and Thatcher's shattered Britain had been the main topics. It was still way too early to go down to Dave's, as he was out working with his old man, so I set about matching the new lyrics with the new guitar riffs. It was a bit hit-and-miss to start with, some riffs and lyrics matching up quickly, while others would have to wait to find their matches. I soon found some new Virus V1 track material, so I turned my attention away from the embryonic stage of track writing to my favourite part of the process, which was seeing how they would sound by putting together a new Test Tape. 'Let your slaves go', 'Pathetic' and 'I.R.A. Ireland' went down easily as the first three tracks on the tape, which was a good strong start to Test Tape Nineteen. I sat back, made a roll-up, sparked it up, listening, thinking about what could be improved.

In amongst the punk and disorderly, the memory of Clare came back to me, rising to the surface, taking me to a better place. So just for a laugh, I stopped trying to put the world to rights for a moment, dropped the polotrix and recorded a punk version of Gilbert O'Sullivan's track 'Clair' changing the lyrics to. 'Clare, the moment I met you, I swear, even though I was Joey in a wheelchair, I felt as if something, somewhere had happened to me, I was pissed on snakebites, you on voddy. Joey and Jolea should have added to the Deacon family tree'. I played it back thinking this could be hilarious, but by the time it had got halfway through, I thought it was probably the worst piece of shit I had written in my life; not as bad as the original, but shit none the same. It even made The Sods sound good, so I rewound the tape back to the start, pressed play/record and erased it before anyone else could hear it, which was another beauty of the Test Tape method, if you wrote shite; simple, rewind, press play/record, goodbye shite.

I was on top of the world by the time I set off for Dave's later that afternoon; I couldn't have felt any better, it was like the whole world had been made for me, for me to enjoy. In the sky above, light clouds slid gently along on an azure background, the sun nosing at their edges, warming me, warming the world, as I went down my road past Doggy's quiet tomb-like abode - there were no lights on, but there were people home. I strolled easily through the two white fences at the side of Hilary's tip of a house, where I saw another poor action man had been torched, burnt beyond recognition, an acceptable loss, sacrificed to a god unknown, moving eyes unmoving, glazed over searching fruitlessly for meaning in his empty sky.

A car started up at the front of his house, I sped up a bit grinning at the memory of gravel showering through his open car window. The muffled holler as the flint, chert, and chalk connected with the vengeful clergyman's face, after we took his car for an impromptu spin up my road. I thought, where was your god then? Oh yeah, he may watch over your flocks by night, but not over your mud-stained Citroen CX, you bloody nutjob.

Into the churchyard I ambled, where I saw a cloud of insects gambling on an early spring, the swarm shiny, undulating, drifting on a gentle breeze, passed by me on a wing and a prayer, going in the direction of the welcoming Williams household, and I followed in their wake.

In the kitchen, stood Dave, like he had been waiting there all night, wanting to know if the Deaconite had finally got himself a girlfriend, or had he, by any chance, fucked it up, again.

"You alright?" Dave grinned. "What happened Skin?" He asked., even before I could return his greeting.

I snorted lasciviously, "Come on, let's go and have a few pints, I'll tell you."

Dave nodded, grabbed his leather jacket, and we set off down the hill for the pub. I told him in the rapidly waning daylight, how Clare and me had got on so well together, how she had bought the drinks for most of the night, how I thought he and Phil might have fucked it up for me, and finally how we had fucked in the house across the road from The Anchor.

Dave creased up, "Bloody hell, you fucked her in the empty house!"

"Yeah... Well, she brought the drinks for most of the night, it was the least I could do!"

"You know Don Ruddock bought that house, don't you? It's Don's house you fucked in."

"Er... No... No, I didn't..." I said, thinking, oh shit I could be in trouble here, then after a quick re-think, I thought I couldn't give a shit. I'm on top of the world today, "I tell you what Dave, he's done well there, it's got a lovely original fireplace and a Butler sink in the kitchen."

"Oooh how lovely," said Dave sarcastically. "It sounds like you did well there, Skin, she's a beautiful girl, and she brought all the drinks as well?"

"Yeah, she got me drunk and had her wicked way with me, I just feel so used," I joked, pretending to wipe the tears from my eyes, sending us both into fits of laughter.

"I just feel so used," repeated Dave, slapping his hand onto his forehead.

"I do mate, I don't normally go the whole way on the first date, maybe a quick hand shandy, that's it… she got me so drunk… I would have probably fucked The Soup Dragon."

Dave led the way into the pub, still laughing at his poor mate 'being used' and headed straight for the bar, where he ordered a couple of pints to kick the evening off with, a snakebite for me and a lager for himself, which would do nicely. Stewart watched my every move as he pulled on the tap and the refreshing alcohol filled the gleaming glasses in front of him. If you're going to say something, I thought, fucking say something or fuck off you knobend, this sharp-look routine is getting boring. It was like he read my mind and turned his full attention to his job, making sure every last drop of the precious juice landed where it should do, in my glass, so I turned too, surveying the pub. It was early, maybe six o'clock, there weren't many in yet, Craig and Taddy were playing darts in our bar, watched over by Ski Sunday, Lucy Flat Chesterman, Coops and Mal, while Danny, Ronnie, Lee and Glyn were sitting in the snug in the main bar near us, leaning into each other, chatting avidly, all business like.

Danny looked over at us. "You alright Skinner," he said, grinning, beckoning us over.

Dave and me exchanged a glance, shrugged our shoulders, picked up our drinks, sauntered over.

"What are yous two up to?" Danny asked.

Dave pounced, "We're having a shit, what's it look like we are doing."

Danny ignored him, "No I mean later; we're going to get some whiskey."

"Yeaaahhh? Tell us about it," said Dave sarcastically.

"Oh what, this should be good, come on then Danny what's this all about," I asked, setting down my fresh pint onto the table in the middle of the snug.

Danny raised his eyebrows at the others who grinned back, knowingly, and while we drank deeply, he told us that he'd been doing a bit of gardening work at old man Dawkins's place, up at the top of Ermine Street and when he was putting the tools away at the end of the day, he'd seen 'a box of whiskey' in the garage. Dave and me both creased up laughing.

"A box of whiskey!?" Dave said, sarcastically.

I snorted, "What was it in cubes?" I suggested, wiping froth from my lips.

Dave creased up, "Yeah cubes of Whiskey, big in the wine bars I heard, bloody hell."

"I mean… A box… With bottles of whisky in it," Danny countered.

"Oh OK… So, you saw the bottles of whisky in this box?" Dave asked.

Danny picked up his lager, "Yeah well, there were bottles inside the box which said whisky on it, so they must be whisky bottles." He said, using Danny logic.

"Oh, leave it out Danny, there could be anything in them, holy water, piss, my piss, your piss, anything," Dave replied incredulously.

Danny waved his concerns away, "What do you reckon then Dave, are you in?"

Dave glared at the unblinking Danny, repeated, "Are you in?" Heavily, slowly shaking his head in disbelief at the front of the bloke, "Dear, oh dear, oh dear."

Ronnie cackled; Dave swung around on him, "Oh yeah, so are you in then, Ronnie?"

Ronnie eyed him, sniffed, slouched back in his chair, took a drag on his cigarette. "I'm in," he said, ostentatiously blowing a smoke ring towards Dave.

Dave swatted it away aggressively, "Who do you think you are? Mr. fucking T?"

"Jesus. The cheeky bastard," he said irritably, turning to me.

"Mr. T.U.R.D. more like," I said, cracking up.

Dave laughed, his eyes swivelling back to Ronnie, pinning him to his seat, daring him to say something else, or blow another fucking smoke ring at him.

"What about yous two?" Danny asked, giving up on Dave, looking to Lee and Glyn.

"We're in," they replied in unison.

I thought about it for a moment. "Yeah, me too, I'm up for it," I said, surprising everyone.

Dave shot me a look, "Oh come on Skin, really?"

I nodded slowly, "I fucking hate Dawkins, you remember when he caught me scrumping apples in his orchard, he grabbed me, gave me a proper fucking hiding mate, bounced me off an apple tree, I was only eight years old, you remember? And when my old man went round there to complain the wanker said he'd do it again too."

It was all on Dave now, he slowly nodded, looked down, shook his head, grimaced. "Hmmm, I don't know Skin, you can't trust anything he says," he acquiesced, giving Danny a cursory glance.

No you can't, I thought, but I don't care. It sounds like a laugh, and it would be good to get even with that bullying asshole Dawkins after all these years,

"Come on Dave it'll be a laugh, let's go and have a look and if it looks dodgy, we'll walk away and let Mr. T.U.R.D here sort it out," nodding towards the still nervous-looking Ronnie.

Dave thought about it for a moment and said, "OK," without much enthusiasm.

Danny sat back, rubbing his hands together, elated, "I love it when a plan comes together."

I thought, fucking hell, we are the A-Team after all.

In the pub the pints came and went, outside, the street lights along the A10 flickered on like fireflies in bottles as the golden evening sun disappeared over the horizon of High Cross Hill, and we saw dusk was settling in, bringing with it the long shadows of the end of the day. I was pissed, so was Dave, we were all pissed, it was time to go. Danny or John 'Hannibal' Smith, as we had started calling him, gave us all the nod. I nodded back, drained my pint, thinking whatever happens here, I don't give a shit I'm on top of the world and while I'm here at the summit, I'm going to put things right for once. OK, I had been on Dawkins's property nicking his apples, but a fully grown man laying into an eight-year-old like that. No I'm not having that, I'm having his whisky and anything else I can get my hands on too, the bastard.

Danny led us, his crack commando unit out of the pub, and up the A10, chewing on an old roll-up like it was a cigar, talking like he was special forces, sounding like he was special needs. Dave kept on looking at me like he was wondering when I was going to tell him that it was a wind up, and we should get back to The Anchor to carry on where we had left off. I said nothing, though, I was determined that a bullying asshole was getting to get his comeuppance tonight, so through the incoming darkness, we drunkenly weaved our way up to Dawkins's place.

Once we got near to the front of the property, we silently dropped down behind some shrubs, to check the place out, see what was what. A single light at the back of the house shone out illuminating the orchard behind the property, every other light was off, it was all quiet on the Dawkins front. I thought we don't need to be special forces here, special needs will suffice, even a pissed-up A team could liberate all that beautiful alcohol without killing a soul.

Danny gave me a nod, I grinned back at him and signalled the OK to Dave, who looked away nervously up the street watching for any movement. It couldn't have been simpler for me though, the garage was at the front of the house and there before us lay a short drive surrounded by a thick matt of bushes, leading from Ermine Street, up to that garage, it was time.

"Let's go," said Danny, cackling to himself.

"Yeah, let's go," I said, bouncing up way too quickly making my head spin,

I took a deep breath, shook it off, dropped to my haunches and light-footedly made my way across Ermine Street and up the covered drive, with Danny following close behind.

In the garden, amongst the herbaceous borders standing high around me, I felt safe, it was a proper shield, I doubted anyone could have seen us from the house, even if they looked out of the front window, and if it wasn't for Danny's incessant sniggering, I doubted anyone could have heard us either. Danny sneaked up to the up-and-over garage door, gave it an almighty tug, but the lock held fast, clanking noisily, sending us sprawling to our knees in fits of laughter.

"Nice one, Danny, how the fuck are we supposed to get in?" I asked through a mouthful of laughter.

"Ring the doorbell?" Came his answer.

"Fuck off, man," my answer came back, cracking us both up again, "Nah, seriously, Danny, how are we going to get in?"

Danny shrugged his shoulders, "I don't know, that's the entrance I use."

"Oh what, great, you're not Hannibal, you're not even Hanna Barbera."

"What's a Hanna Barbera?"

"It's a cartoon co... it doesn't matter."

I slapped my head, thought back to the pub, 'you can't trust anything he says, Skin'. Dave's wise words came back to me.

"Nah this is getting stupid Danny, come on mate, if we don't start taking this seriously, we're going to get fucking nicked, I'll check the side, there must be a side door," I said, looking back to see if the others were following, and there at the bottom of the drive was Ronnie standing under a street light, lit up like a Christmas tree.

I hissed, "Stupid fucking twat,"

Danny waved irritably at him to get down, and after waving back like a Navy wife waving her Jack Tar off to sea, the Muppet finally flopped down behind a bush to his side.

In front of us a bedroom light switched on, throwing its light onto the drive behind us, and we froze, waiting for any other movement, there wasn't any, so ignoring the urge to laugh at Danny's lopsided grinning white teeth shining back at me out of the blackness. I ducked down low and stalked around the garage and immediately found a side door.

"Ronnie's standing up again, Skinner," Whispered Danny's pearly whites.

"I don't care."

One door separated me from a whole box of free booze, so I wasn't hanging about, I fumbled for the handle in the dim light, found it, gently twisted, pulled and the door seemed to break its seal, creakily jerking open, a quick look behind me, and I cautiously made my way inside.

A smell of petrol and grass cuttings greeted my nostrils in the enclosed space of the garage, suddenly it felt several degrees colder. I breathed deeply searching for oxygen, but the damp, musty air around me in the enclosed space could not circulate, it was trapped, languid. To the right of me, on the main doors two pillar-box-type windows cast shards of light onto the white concrete floor beneath my feet, which was a relief, as without them, I wouldn't have been able to see the nose on my face. In the corner of the garage there was a workbench and in amongst the various garden tools and boxes there was a light-brown box with Glen Fiddich whisky written in red letters on the side of it, and I moved in to claim my well-earned prize. I picked it up, took the box to one of the shards, looked inside and saw there were three bottles of tonic water, a bottle of Appletizer and an empty milk bottle.

A couple of other boxes nearby revealed a party four-pack of coke, a bottle of cider and a family bag of Cheesy Wotsits, so tossing the Cheesy Wotsits aside, I grabbed my meagre haul and turned to make my escape. I stopped, took a deep breath, there to the left of me was another door going from the garage into the house, fuck it I thought, while I'm here, let's have a look around, see if there's anything really worth nicking, so I put my meagre swag box down, sidled up the door and waited, listening. I heard nothing, so opened it carefully, still listening all the time for any movement, and still hearing nothing, I ventured tentatively into the house, tiptoeing carefully across a plush wooden-floored hallway and found myself looking into the front room. It smelt of ash, cigar smoke and was musty like the garage had been.

Once my eyes had become accustomed to the dingy light finding its way around a thick curtained window to my right, I saw there was an open fireplace- hence the deep smell of ash and above the hearth, on a York Stone mantelpiece stood an expensive-looking carriage clock ticking away the seconds back at me unconcernedly. Basher had told me that some carriage clocks were worth a few quid, as 'they have gold leaf on them so if you see the gold, nick them any chance you get.' I made my way over, picked it up, scrutinized it carefully- I didn't know what I was looking at. It looked like gold, but I didn't know. I placed it back onto the mantelpiece, only to feel it falling forwards, so scrabbling at it with both hands I plucked it out of the air, and with a feeling of relief, planted it solidly back in its place and scanned the room again.

On an elaborate table under the window sat a large, globe-shaped drinks cabinet, the top opened up like a cracked egg, revealing an array of different bottles, it was loaded, there must have been a dozen, maybe more. I thought, that's more like it, we are going to get something decent after all, and fast walked over to the gaping orb, grabbed a couple of bottles up grinning like a wanker perusing the top shelf in a newsagent's and then above me the ceiling creaked beneath someone's body weight, and my grin stalled, someone was on the move, someone heavy was on the move. I gaped up watching the ceiling, tracing the movement, my heart racing, whoever it was, they were moving with purpose, moving with purpose, towards the middle of the house, towards the stairs. Oh shit, I thought, I've got to get out of here, so I shoved the bottles carelessly back into the globe, they clinked loudly as they fell and legged it back across the hall and stopped abruptly outside garage. Oh no. Nooo, someone was moving around in there too, and not trying to hide the fact either, meanwhile whoever it was upstairs, was rapidly descending the stairs.

No way forward, no way back I was trapped- I froze, my heart pounding out of my chest, thumping in my ears, blood shooting oxygen around my body, making me ready for anything, fight or flight, fight or flight, fight or flight. I'm not ready for anything, fight or flight, I thought, oh shit, shit, shit, the panic rising inside me, Jesus Christ, fucking trapped, nowhere to run to, nowhere to hide. I'm not eight years old now, I'll show the bastard, let's get this over with, do it now, there was nothing else I could do. I rammed the door to the garage open with my shoulder, gritted my teeth, drew back my fist and there was Danny standing there gawping at me.

Danny put his hand on his heart. "Oh, fucking hell, I thought you were old man Dawkins; what are you doing in there? You mad bastard!" He said out of breath.

"I'm fucking mad alright, mad for listening to you…
You knobend, there's no fucking whisky in here!"

Danny grinned lopsidedly, producing a bottle of wine from out of the darkness like a magician.

"OK, nice one, mate, we need to…"

"I love it when a plan comes together, look at this, it's a fruity red… I saw it under a bag of family- sized Wotsits, I didn't think there was anything in there and then…"

"Er… Danny we need to go."

"I chucked the Wotsits out of the way, who likes those things? They stink like a used jock strap, then I saw a bottle of wine in one of those weird beams of light, so I grabbed it.

"Danny, shut up mate, we need to get the fuck out of here NOW, old man Dawkins is coming."

"Oh shit, I was wondering what was going on, I thought you were……"

I had to act fast, so I pushed the rambling fool towards the door.

"FUCKING NOW!" I bellowed.

Danny finally got the message, and we disappeared off into the night.

Chapter 6

The Cannon and Ball Show

I was having a rare night in; my mates had been more than generous in lining up the snakebites for me over the past week, so I decided to give The Anchor a miss. It was OK having a couple pints off them, but I didn't want to take the piss. In a couple of days, I would put things right again, as I was due a Giro from the lovely people at the SOSH, and Mrs. Gruber, the old widow I did a bit of gardening for was visiting relatives back in Germany, owed me for a week's money too, so it wouldn't be too long until I was back in the land of the living again. It was boring staying in at night, that's when things happened, good things, things that I wanted to do every night, like smoking, drinking, and if the chance came along, break into a house and fuck Clare, one of the most beautiful girls in the village. On a night inside, I always wondered what everyone was doing, what I was going to miss, and maybe, just maybe, she would be there in The Anchor. Clare Rapunzel, the translucent girl would find a way to free herself from her tower, return to me, and once more we could undress, and lose ourselves in the orange glow of the street lights.

I thought at the time, it would only be a one-night stand, but why should it be? OK, she was living in a different world to me. A world of Yuppies and Tories, but so what? Who cares? We could keep it quiet from the people who would be disappointed in Clare's choice; all that needed to happen is for her to dodge her wanker of a stepdad and come to The Anchor. I would ask her out and see what happens, if she says yes, great, we'll head to Deacon Cottage. If no, then at least I'll know… What if she says 'I don't know, I'll think about it', or more likely 'I'd like too, but it's complicated', then what, I'd be out in the open, do I want to leave myself open? Look like, some love-sick puppy twat, waiting, forever waiting... Round and round, it went in my head, until it became torturous, just thinking about the milliard of different scenarios with all their variables.

In the end, I reasoned, it was a Sunday night; she wouldn't be there even if she escaped The Pillock, and surely, I couldn't be missing too much on a wintery Sunday night in The Anchor, could I? Nah, no way, and as much as I hated staying in. Mum and the old man seemed to like it, and had already made plans for my night's incarceration, after the old man had read in the Radio Times that there was something about the 'pop world' on the consumer program 'That's Life'. I must admit, as he told me, I thought that sounds boring - societies A-Z of being a wanker with a guitar, what a waste of my time - but after some gentle persuasion from mum. I cleared my mind, took the cynical look off my face and settled down with them to watch Esther Rantzen and that weird boss-eyed bloke Cyril Fletcher talking bollocks from his comfy chair. It turned out that it wasn't a waste of my time after all, as I was finding inspiration for my music everywhere since the new year and a few yawns into the show, during one of That's Life's oh so heart-warming, life affirming investigative parts, where pensioners Albert and Dolly Smedley, had taken on British Gas for over-charging them, even though they didn't have gas, yawn. I heard an amazing piece of incidental music that made the hairs on the back of my neck stand up.

Once I had worked out what I thought the root notes of the piece of music might be in my head, I needed to get to my guitar quickly before I forgot them. So I decamped to my bedroom, leaving my mum to tut over the injustice of it all and my old man to carry on fantasying about Esther. Inside the sanctuary of my bedroom, as always, the music world opened up in front of me, I felt like I could play anything, and it would sound good. It was a world I was happiest in. I grabbed up my guitar, sat down on my bed, and soon worked out the notes - it was a sort of Spanish progression of F#, E and G. I messed around with the chords, chopping and changing their order until I liked what I heard, then, when I liked what I heard, it was time to make it punk rock. I played a dampened F# chord for one bar, hit half a bar for E, then quarter each on F# and E as fast as I could. It was perfect, so I took my scribbles of riffs and lyrics book off my bedside table and set about trying to match it up with some of the other riffs I had waiting, and I found a corresponding riff almost at once. One strike D, one strike C, half a bar B#, then one full bar of A was perfect for the chorus- it was all coming together nicely. If it had been the early days of Virus V1, I would have considered the music part of the track finished until we worked it through as a band, but I didn't feel the same now. I was trying to make our tracks more elaborate, experimenting with intros, middle eights, bridges and even tempo changes.

Virus V1 had played a huge gig, in front of a lot of people. It felt like our time was coming, and when it did, I thought we would need something different, something to set us apart from the rest of that bands out there. We could out-thrash any of them, but we needed to be more than a verse, chorus punk band, we needed progress, to move forward, and if I wrote more complicated track ideas now, at their inception, then later, together as a band. Andy, Whiff Dave, and me could work on them and turn them into something really impressive and ultimately lasting.

On this new track, a middle eight would be perfect, and as the verse, chorus part of it was fast, a slow middle eight would be great. A slow grinding middle eight, then a build-up ... I was brought back to reality by the sound of our doorbell ringing downstairs; an unusual occurrence at any time, particularly in the evening, nobody called at our house except Andy, Whiff and Dave, and I knew they were all busy. Whiff was on the piss with Custer Cowling and his soul boy mates. Andy was at his boxing club punching the shit out of someone, and Dave was out with Steph probably having a scrap too, either that, or having the kind of intensive sex that I could only dream of. I stopped playing, craned my neck, and listened. A moment of silence passed, and I was just about to start grinding the middle eight again, when I heard my mum shout,

"Mike!?"

Clare, it's Clare, oh my, it's Clare, my heart sang. Clare!! It's not fucking Clare, you knobend, my head replied, giving me a bit of clarity.

"MIKE!!!" She shouted, insistently.

Mum wasn't going away, not this time anyway, so I rolled my eyes, sighed irritably, propped my guitar against the wall, keys out, thinking fucking hell, what is it now? How can I write music if I'm being disturbed all the time? I bet Steve Ignorant, or Cal out of Discharge, doesn't have to put up with their mum shouting upstairs for them all the time, while they're writing. Oh well. I left the sanctum of my bedroom, the music world vanished, and there she was, my mum at the bottom of stairs, eyes wide like saucers, looking up anxiously, questioningly, worried.

"It's the police," she whispered.

Oh what, what do those wankers want, I thought? And then oh yeah... I know exactly what those wankers want... Oh shit.

"Yeah, OK, I'm coming."

I snatched up a couple of ready-made roll-ups out of the mess on my bedside table, gingerly made my way downstairs and there he was, standing in my hallway, piled up high like a mound of pig shit. P.C Cannon, the long snout of the law - the long snout of the law, in my house!!! Cannon held his tit head helmet firmly in the crook of his arm, steadily pursuing my mum's stunned face, he nodded at the old man who joined my mum at the door, then turned his attention to the sound of footsteps on the stairs, saw me falter, and a broad grin ploughed its way across his face, telling me, that every pig has its day.

P.C. Cannon wasn't alone either, he had brought back up with him this time, out of the shadows, stepped his partner, ostentatiously sweeping off his peaked cap he introduced himself as Peter Ball of the youth liaisons group, shaking my old man's hand solidly, like he was saying I'm the boss now, the old man knew it to be true. I didn't, though, I thought I had misheard him. Peter Ball? I stifled a laugh and thought there has to be some kind of mistake here, surely this is some kind of joke, isn't it? Cannon and Ball? Cannon and Ball like the comedy duo on TV as in 'Rock on Tommy'. It took all of my will power not to burst out laughing then and there as their moronic catchphrases came back to me, filling my helpless head, 'I'm dead excited', 'You little liar', and then the crème de la creme for this evening 'You ate me, don't yer?'

Mum hadn't noticed, I was surprised, as she always had an eye for the ridiculous, laughed at the same things as me. I took a glance at her; she wasn't laughing, far from it, she looked old and tired now, deep lines of worry scarring her face, I thought oh shit, I checked the old man, and his expression sat somewhere between fuming anger and intense confusion, I thought surely this isn't that serious, is it? We were pissed up. It was only a laugh, well, that and levelling up with old man Dawkins for the beating he gave me when I was a kid, so where was the Cannon and Ball show then? I bet if I had told them, they would have said 'You little liar' - bastards.

"What can we do for you, officers?" My old man started, trying to take back some kind of control in his own house.

"We need to have a word with Michael, it might take some time… Is there anywhere we could sit down, please?" Peter Ball announced, all dour and business-like, taking complete control.

The old man nodded minutely, retreating, leading them into the front room, mum shuffling silently behind him, like a blind beggar.

"Sit down officers," said the old man, hands out, magnanimously.

Peter Ball nodded, and sat down heavily in my old man's chair, not realising it was a rocking chair and it tottered backwards precariously.

"Ooooowwwhhh!" He said, throwing his feet up in the air to balance it before it went over.

The chair reached maximum rock, then lurched forwards righting itself.

"Oooh oh, ha, ha, yes … It's a rocking chair" he simpered, now safe back on terra firma, self-consciously aware that everyone in the room was watching him, the face of authority, looking like a dimwit, and he grinned idiotically back at us all.

'Rock on Tommy' I thought and once again suppressed an urge to laugh out loud at this tosser, making a tosser of himself in my front room.

It was silent in the room while he stabilized himself, regained his composure, then back in control now he solemnly slid a light-blue notebook out of a small attaché case at his side, slipped a pen out of his top pocket and looked up expectantly at Cannon, who was getting comfortable on my settee, in my lounge, in my house, the wanker.

"We are very busy, as I'm sure you are Mr. and Mrs. Baker, so I'm not going to beat about the bush here, last Sunday evening, there was a burglary in the village, now, we've spoken to Danny O' Shea, Phil Buttercroft, Richard O'Keefe, David Williams and Glyn and Lee Walker, and they all say that they were there,"

"Were you there, Michael?"

Peter Ball enquired, his eyes burning into mine like they were trying to suck the truth out.

Oh, fucking hell I thought, they've spoken to everyone. I looked down, trying to think of the right thing to say, found myself getting lost in the patterns on my mum's home-made Persian rug. It took her ages to make that, maybe a year working hard every night, pushing the latch hook tool, filling the holes with her bright colours, even when she didn't want to, she would do a little bit more. It was like a labour of love to her; she knew it would be worth it in the end.

"Nah I wasn't there; I don't know what you are talking about," I said finally, raising my head.

P.C. Cannon smiled, "Oh dear, oh dear, don't deny it, we know you were there, everyone said you were, this is just what I was saying sir, he is…"

Peter Ball held his hand up, consulted his notebook, "OK, OK, it's fine officer Cannon, I'll bring this one in. Michael, we have a witness that says that you left The Anchor pub around six o'clock with David Williams, Danny O'Shea, Phil Buttercroft, Richard O'Keefe, Glyn and Lee Walker, after having some drinks and went directly to Orchard Cottage in Ermine Street, yes?" His head swivelling between my mum and the old man, looking for more back up.

On hearing no reply, Ball thumped his notebook onto his knees angrily, "Michael, it's up to you, I don't mind, we can either do this here or we can do it down at the station, but believe me, if we do have to go to the station to sort this out, you will be interviewed under caution, and with the evidence that we have, the CPS will charge you with burglary, you will, end up in court."

I looked to my mum's home-made rug, the colours so painstakingly put together.

Peter Ball sighed, "OK last chance, were you there?"

Mum had, had enough now. "Oh, for god's sake, MIKE!" She shouted.

I looked up, away from the warmth of the colours, back to the grey reality, "Phil Buttercroft wasn't there; he wasn't anything to do with it."

"But you were though?" Countered Peter Ball.

"Yeah, I was there," I admitted, feeling disgusted with myself, knowing the elation that fucking Tamworth Pig Cannon must be feeling now.

"OK, good, right, you made the right decision Michael, if we had gone to the station, your life would have changed, for the worst I can tell you. I've seen young men like yourself try and play the tough guy, show their misplaced loyalty and end up in jail."

Peter Ball nodded self-righteously, began writing in his notebook.

A smoke seemed like a good idea at that moment, so I took a ready-made roll up from behind my ear, chucked it between my lips, sparked it, trying to avoid the look on my mum's face. I didn't need to look. I knew what it said. It said why? It said betray. It said you bloody fool, and worst of all, it said I trusted you. I trusted you, and you go and do a stupid thing like this? You've let yourself down, you've let me down, you've hurt me, hurt me badly.

Once Peter Ball had finished scribbling away, he calmly replaced his light blue notebook into his case at his side, then shifting his weight carefully on the rocking chair he told the old man and mum exactly what we had done. I sat back and listened in wonder as every detail emerged; it was like the bastards had been in on it themselves. On and on he went. So much so, that I started to get bored, zoned out. I blew a huge nimbus cloud of smoke in the direction of Cannon who was grinning, loving every minute of it. He was nodding along sycophantically to his superior like a nodding dog on a car's back rack on a particularly bumpy road, as his points hit home.

P.C. Cannon paused, dropped his head under my smoke screen, tutted, unconcerned with the little punk's games, now he was bang to rights, and just carried on nodding at the story, which seemed to be going on longer than the actual 'burglary'.

I was suddenly all ears when Ball said "…The occupant said he heard someone in the garage and was frightened…" "… He didn't think anyone had come into the house, if that had been the case, all the assailants would have been arrested, and we would be doing this at the police station…" I nodded my head along with the Angeln saddleback, Cannon on that one.

Oh well, I got away with that, I thought smirking inwardly; Cannon and Ball living up to their names, a couple of comedians in crackling - what a couple of Keystone cocks.

"…In the course of our investigations…" he continued, "We received information from one of the younger children in the village that Richard O'Keefe was involved, so we went to see him and told him that 'We know what you've been up to, tell us about it? And thankfully for everyone concerned, he did, he told us all we needed to know …"

Ronnie, you wanker, I thought, you fell for the oldest trick in the book. 'I'm in" you said. You wait till I fucking catch up with you, your face is going to be 'in' – fucking kicked in.

Peter Ball turned on me, "OK now Michael, you've been lucky this time, and from the information we have received, you have been on many previous occasions too. It has to stop... I am warning you now, this is it, this is your last chance. When we catch you next time, and let me assure you, we will catch you, you will be arrested, and you will go to court. And let me tell you... If it's anything of this kind of magnitude, you can expect a custodial sentence."

Peter Bell let his words sink in, then, carefully rocked the chair forward, scrutinizing me like I should be hung by the neck till dead, he wasn't finished yet. "Personally, I think because of the serious nature of this crime, you should be arrested and taken to court." he said, to Cannon, his side-kick, who broke from his rhythmical nodding and nodded back at him concisely.

I thought at any moment the dim-witted Tamworth's head might disconnect altogether, it had been wobbling around so much, however, his neck was strong, and his toad-like display of subservience was nowhere near over, and he soon found his rhythm again.

"And you would have been too, if it hadn't been for certain adults in the village speaking up for you," he said, standing up, looking over to PC Cannon, and he did the same.

"OK right... Before we go, I would also like to warn you Michael that once you get a criminal record, it stays with you forever, and it might affect your chances of getting a job in future."

Oh well, I thought, getting a criminal record's not so bad after all then, anything that keeps me out of the fucking mouse race. A feeling of great relief washed over me as I watched my old man jump up and lead the edgy family teatime comedy duo out. I sat back, lit another roll-up and braced myself, ready for the inevitable assault my old man was going to give me on his return.

Mum wasn't waiting for him, she was incensed, her eyes blazed, she spat, "I don't know about you sometimes Mike, you've got a screw loose somewhere, what is wrong with you? You strut around posing all the time in your silly clothes, trying to show everyone that you're different from everyone else, like you've got better morals than everyone else, well you're not, and you haven't, you're just a bloody yobbo, Mike," she shouted.

I had no answer to that, I sat stunned, like I had been hit by a truck, if mum said that to me then I must have done something bad, really bad, it was Dawkins, though, surely it didn't count.

"Whatever possessed you? Why do such a thing?" Mum asked from the depths of her broken heart.

"I don't know mum, it just happened."

Mum snorted, "Oh, give it a rest for god's sake."

A few moments later, the old man's livid face came and joined in barrage, "What did you do that for?"

I had had enough myself, "It was old man Dawkins, wasn't it? You remember when he hit me when I was a little kid? The old bastard really laid into me and you went round there, and he said he'd do it again… You remember, you said the Dawkins family looked down their noses at us."

"Oh yeah, here we go again, if I've told you once, I've told you a thousand times, don't try to bullshit a bullshitter," said the old man, nodding, smiling.

Mum gaped at the ease with which I had diverted the old man's attention away from the real issue, I throw a bit of family loyalty, his way, back him up, and all is forgotten, not this time though, this was a burglary, this was the police. It had gone way too far for that.

"For the love of god Mike, that's no excuse, you don't walk into someone's house like that," she huffed, angrily firing eyes at the old man, whose smile vanished.

"I didn't go in their house, it was only the garage," I lied.

Mum stood up, "In their house, in their garage, in their garden, wherever, you don't go on someone else's property, and stealing too, you'd better start sorting yourself out, Mike, I've had it up to here with you." Her anger rising with her.

"Yeah, yeah, yeah, bollocks to this, I've had a lecture from the old bill, I've had enough now I'm going upstairs," I said, rising back at her.

Mum shouted, "Yes, yes, yes, go then, get out of my sight."

My old man added, "Yeah and stay up there, you little bastard, or I'll kick a bloody great hole through you," as I departed.

I went upstairs to the sanctuary of my bedroom, a room of music, of something I could understand, a place of only right and wrong, good music and bad. I sat down heavily on my bed, listening to mum and the old man's raised voices from downstairs throwing the blame one way then the other, like they thought they were responsible for my actions. It was my life, my actions and therefore the consequences of those actions would be mine, not theirs, they'd had their lives, done what they wanted to do, followed their dreams till they became just that, dreams. If it didn't happen for them like they wanted it, too, why take it out on me? I'm not to blame. I cued up Virus V1 Live at Richard Hole on my tape recorder, zoned out; I'd heard it all before, only this time the catalyst was an almost burglary. It wasn't the great train robbery, I thought, only a bottle of wine, and a couple of bottles of Appletise, for fucks sake we didn't even take the family bag of Wortzits, we left the fat bastard something. I snorted, lit another roll-up, took a decent puff, inhaled deeply to let the nicotine heal and replenish my aching head, then lay back on my bed and thought 'Cannon and Ball', chuckling to myself, how could no one have noticed that.

Chapter 7

And Stop Smoking That Marijuana in Your Bedroom

On most mornings since the old man had retired, we would have breakfast together, chatting, talking about anything and everything apart from politics, that is, as we both knew where that would lead; a full-on argument with doors slammed, followed by stony silences. I wasn't going to change my morning routine just because of recent events, and it seemed like he wasn't going to either, so I followed him downstairs at the usual time of nine o'clock and braced myself for another lecture from him, and yet another 'you need to sort your life out speech' from mum.

In fact, I need not have worried, as they were both giving me the silent treatment - mum buried her head deep in a book, while the old man hid behind his broadsheet - which suited me just fine. I had heard all their bullshit a million times before, over the years since I had left school. Mum's hysterical pleas for me to make a plan B, to give me 'something to fall back on if the music didn't happen' and funnier still, the old man's dour predictions that I would end up destitute. On the streets of London begging, spending my nights with the other winos, curled up, sleeping under Hungerford bridge, if I didn't straighten up and fly right. I mean, what was he on about? Hungerford bridge spanned the River Thames. I'd need a fucking Lilo to sleep under there.

On and on they went, Hungerford, Plan B, Hungerford, Plan B, it was like a closed groove on a record. I couldn't be bothered with it. It was just a pack of lies, a ruse, a way to get me to succumb, be a good little boy, do what you're told, behave or the bad big wolf called life will get you. If they didn't want to talk, fine, I had more important things to think about than selling my arse or whatever shit they said was waiting for me 'in the real world'. Whiff was coming round in the afternoon and I wanted to go through the new track I had been working on; that was what I was doing, that was my future. Not working like a slave on a farm for some overseer boss, or for some hot headed, weak-hearted Disney abomination like Geppetto, mending and polishing shoes or just polishing them, if they didn't need mending. Fuck that, give me a Lilo.

Whiff had the route notes already; knowing his enthusiasm for the band, he would have been practising, refining them, putting his touch on them, so I knew that he would be more than ready to go. I had a nice surprise for him, too. My gypsy mate Ashley, had come through for me with a nice little bag of sensi - a lay on till the Sosh came through for me - so we would have a nice inspirational smoke as we worked. Whiff and me both agreed, that grass helped to focus the mind, especially where music was concerned. It blotted out the bullshit. The distractions, let the inspiration come, especially if it was good, and I knew it would be good, as my mate Ashley had scored it up at The Frontline in Hackney, or herb central as he had called it, between bouts of the giggles.

One spoonful at a time, I slowly shovelled the cornflakes into my mouth in the tomblike atmosphere of the kitchen. It wasn't so bad; it was nice to have a bit of quiet first thing in the morning. It was peaceful, calm, and apart from the gentle hum of the fridge as it kept our dairy products cool, keeping the bacteria at bay, it was completely silent. A time of restful awakeness, before the day began. George appeared at the back door after a night of mousing, and even he didn't raise much of a reaction from the silent two. I stifled a laugh, watching the ginger and white miracle cat standing on his hind legs paddling insistently on the back door glass using his front paws.

I snorted, chucked my spoon down, went to the door and let him in, and he darted to his bowl and tucked into the meat and tasty gravy - still nothing from the old man and mum. I thought, well there's no need to take it out on the cat, he didn't do anything, fuck this, and gave the tomblike two one more brief glance, then grabbed my leather jacket, and decamped for Dave's to see how he was fairing after his visit from Cannon and Ball, the not-so, dynamic duo.

On the walk down, not surprisingly, I found it was just another perfect day. Birds sang out their greetings to all and sundry, some spiralling up joyously into the sun above, which blazed down from a cloudless blue sky, reflecting the jewel-like clusters of frost beneath my D.M.s. I wondered what Dave's old man's reaction might have been, I wasn't too worried though, as Dave had told me that he never hit him. In the past when he had stepped out of line, his old man had screamed, shouted, blew himself out, then once he had made his point, that would be the end of it, he'd leave it, and move on. A line seemed to have been crossed this time, though. It was a 'burglary', 'a serious crime', police officers had invaded people's houses, invaded their privacy. Words like 'arrests', 'court appearances' even 'custodial sentences', had been chucked into the faces of our unsuspecting parents, so who knew what his reaction might be. Lee and Glyn's old man, now that was a worry, the way he was, they would certainly be up for the belt, maybe worse, his reputation for discipline was notorious throughout the village. Ronnie, I didn't know, his old man was passive, a bit slow, even. I hoped he had got it worse than the rest of us, when I caught up with him, he would. I would make sure of it - the whispering grass.

I thought about knocking the door at Dave's in light of recent events, then thought nah, and wandered into Ann's kitchen, just like any other normal day.

"Hello Skinner, have you come to burgle us?" Asked Hayley, greeting me with a wry smile.

It was a normal day, I relaxed.

"Oh, alright Hayley, if you've got anything worth nicking, I will," I replied, grinning from ear to ear, like we had just pulled off the heist of the century.

Hayley threw back her head, laughing. "I bet you would as well," she said, exaggeratedly grabbing silver cutlery off the kitchen table and hiding it under a tablecloth on the pristine side.

Dave appeared behind her from the dining room, playfully pushing her out of the way. "Bloody hell, come on girl mooove," he Alan-ed.

"Oh sorry, I had better go if you two are going to plan your next caper."

"Yeah, you'd better, laav, we're using shooters this time," said Dave, giving her another friendly nudge, this time towards the dining room door.

Hayley laughed, "OK, I wouldn't want to stand in the way of Thundridge's answer to The Kray Twins."

I cackled, watched her go, her blonde hair swaying like a metronome, beautifully in time with its surroundings, captivating me.

Dave shot me a look; I smiled self-consciously, shrugged helplessly, and turned my attention away from the hypnotic blonde locks, looked back to him, looked at his hair. It was different. It wasn't bright red anymore; it was back to normal again – a normal that wasn't so good.

"Oh what, what happened to your hair Dave, was it part of the punishment?"

"I don't know, sort of, I suppose. The old man didn't like it."

I nodded, thinking yeah, he was OK with it a couple of weeks ago, it was part of the punishment.

"He reckoned that if we were going into people's houses doing work for them, it wasn't making a good impression." Dave sighed, opening his arms, he finished, "Well, it's his business, so I can understand it."

I must admit, I was disappointed, really disappointed. Dave looked cool with his red hair, and even though Dave was punk rock in his heart, he didn't really dress punk. It was his visible nod in punks' direction, letting people know.

"Yeah, well, that's right, it is… So how was Pigman Cannon?" I asked, hoping to fill in a few blanks.

"He was a wanker," he said, matter-of-factly.

I snorted, thinking yep.

Dave went on to tell me of his experiences of the day the UK's most famous, edgy teatime family comedy double act had come to call at the Williams household. It was an all too familiar story.
Cannon the wanker sitting on his settee grinning like the Cheshire

cat, revelling in the moment, loving being the harbinger of bad news. Ball all smug and righteous, pontificating from Alan's TV chair, and of course his shocked parents, who could not believe that he had done something so stupid. It was at this point I started to feel guilty, as he wouldn't have done anything so stupid if I hadn't decided to do something so stupid. I was about to apologise when he stopped me in my tracks, by telling me a few things I didn't know. Dave reckoned that they had come to his mid-morning on the Sunday, long before coming to mine, and after he had admitted being there, they charged him with burglary. I couldn't believe it, I gaped at the bloke. I couldn't work out why I hadn't been nicked too, then he told me that after the boys in blue had left, and after Alan had blown his top like Mount Etna. Alan had gone straight round to old man Dawkins' house, persuaded him to withdraw his statement. It took a while, a long while, but once he had, that was the end of it, without a plaintive the police had nothing, they couldn't touch us, so the charges were dropped and Pig Man Cannon's dreams of revenge had been dashed.

I smiled, "I bet the little Tamworth's miserable in his sty this morning."

Dave smirked, "Yeah, I bet he's one sad little piglet this morning."

"One thing though, Dave, did you notice it was Cannon and Ball, like 'you'll do for me Tommy'."

Dave creased up laughing. "Oh yeah, 'rock on Tommy'," he, Bobby Ball-ed.

Dave's face clouded over. "To be honest, no, no I didn't Skin, the words 'you are being arrested for burglary' sort of took my attention," he said, sarcastically.

I looked down, shook my head, pulled a grimace over my smile, "I'm sorry, Dave, I shouldn't have got you involved in that."

"What? I made the decision to come along, you didn't make me, we've been getting away with it for years, we were bound to get caught eventually, it was only a matter of time."

"I suppose," I said, feeling a lot better.

"No, it was a good laugh, watching you two sneaking about in Dawkins' front garden, it was like watching Laurel and Hardy."

"Two Laurels more like Dave, we were both the dim wits."

Dave patted me on the shoulder. "Cannon and Ball, how could I have not seen that?" He asked, chuckling to himself.

"Deep down you really 'ate me don't yer," I Bobby Ball-ed to my best mate, sending us both into spasms of laughter.

Hayley chided, "Shhhhh… I wouldn't let dad hear you two laughing." Returning to the kitchen and right on cue, a huge, seismic Mount Etna-eques shout, rumbled from somewhere deep inside the bowels of the Williams household.

Dave rolled his eyes, "I'd better go."

"OK Dave, you will be at practice this weekend, won't you?"

He gave me a puzzled look, "Oh yeah, I'll be there alright, no doubt about that."

"Nice one Dave, I'll see you then, mate."

I got out of there fast before I too got caught up in the pyroclastic flow.

On the way back up to mine, I began to digest what Dave had told me. It looked like Alan had saved us from the clutches of Her Majesties Pig Force, and we lived to fight another day, another perfect day. It looked like, as far as the authorities were concerned, we had got away with, what the rest of our mates in the village were calling the booze blag. I strolled back into mine, feeling on top of the world again, then I remembered it might be over as far as the authorities were concerned, but in the eyes of my parents it wasn't. Not by a long chalk, they were still stunned, hadn't even begun to think about what my punishment might be. Personally, I was hoping it would be more disappointment and a few more days of the silent routine. I was doubtful, though, so once I had got back to mine, I dodged around the back, sneaked in through the back door into the kitchen, away from the usually busy lounge area, knowing retribution could come at any time. It was all quiet on the kitchen front, so I grabbed a slice of bread, a chunk of cheese and some mixed pickles from the pickle jar, and ghosted up to my room to get ready for an afternoon of my favourite dynamic duo; a bag of sensi and Virus V1.

Once inside the sanctum, I sat down on my bed, picked up my lyric book from the bedside table, began turning its pages, while chomping away on my cheese and pickle sandwich, spraying crumbs down onto my Destroy shirt. I soon found my latest addition, and quietly read out the lyrics I had to go with the 'That's Life' riff I had lifted.

"Spoils of War,

If I die, don't think of me,
I'm dead, gone, lies that shouldn't be,
Never to grow old, bloodline cut,
No glorious resurrection, a hymn book shut,

Victims of a nationalist's plan,
no part of this world will be forever England,

Ashes to ashes, dust is dust,
Metal to rust, metal to rust.

The spoils of war, the spoils of war,

If I die, I won't think of you,
You live, here, heart untrue,
To go on, bloodline told,
Major murderer, lives to grow old,

Victims of a nationalist's plan,
no part of this world will be forever England,

Ashes to ashes, dust is dust,
Metal to rust, metal to rust.

The spoils of war, the spoils of war,"

Whiff wandered into my bedroom, bass in hand, grin on face as I
brushed the cheese and bread flecks onto my bedroom floor.

"Oh what, how did you get in?"

"I rang the doorbell, your mum let me in," said Whiff quizzically, propping his bass against the bed, sitting down, making himself comfortable.

"Yeah, how did she seem?" I asked, relieved that the day of reckoning didn't look like it was going to be today.

Whiff laughed, "Err, same as usual, why? What you been up to Skin?"

I smiled; Whiff was as quick on the uptake as he was on the piss take.

"Er, hold up, first things first…" I said, grabbing my extra-large Rizlas, baccy pouch and a bag of fresh sensi from my secret compartment in the chest of draws next to the open window.

Into the Rizla went a crest of old Holborn, followed by a fat line of herb, while I worked diligently, I ran through the highlights of the booze blag with him. Danny's stupid claim of a box of whiskey. Ronnie's 'I'm in' boast and the smoke ring that Dave swatted out of the air, waiting for darkness to settle in and getting so pissed, we didn't give a shit whether we got caught on not. The lack of whiskey, my walk into the house, almost punching Danny on the way out and of course the Cannon and Ball show waltzing into my house, posturing, threatening, knowing full well that they were powerless after old man Dawkins had taken back his statement.

Whiff's face was a picture throughout as I knew it would be; the surprise, the laughs, the shock, the fear, the incomprehension. Once my construction was complete, I passed him the spliff lit up, and he added serenity to his facial repertoire.

"Fucking hell, you were lucky to get away with that!"

"I don't know if I have yet Whiff, mum and the old man haven't had their say on it yet, there's definitely something coming, I can feel it in the air," I said, plucking the aromatic spliff from Whiff's outstretched hand.

"Yeah, well, there's a lot of bad shit going on at the moment, you remember Mucus?"

"Of course, I do, Marcus Crosswell, the punk at the piss party, I think he was at Bowes too," I said, exhaling a blue cloud.

"Yeah, he was, he was there with his mate Sam, well, him and Sam heard the Newtown Neurotics were a playing a secret gig at The Square in Harlow…"

"I heard about that, there's always rumours going around about them playing secret gigs. I wasn't impressed with them, saw them in Hertford Heath with Chris Dickinson and Basher. Basher nicked half the takings for the gig, just the coins, though… The best part of the night was watching him Toulouse Lautrec-king down the road holding a straining Tesco bag full of coins," I said, cracking up at the memory of the drunken tea-leaf absconding from the scene of the crime, grinning like a fucking maniac.

Whiff put his hand up, "No Skin, this isn't funny mate, seriously, they got a proper kicking, fucking Stampy, Mathews, Moley and their mates jumped them."

Now it was my turn to look shocked, "Oh fuck, what happened man?"

"When they got to the Square there was nobody about, so they hung about for a while, thought fuck it, had a quick drink in the Gene Harlow, then on the way back to the station they cut across an estate… Faircroft, something like that, something Croft, anyway, they walked out into this playing field, stopped next to this little kids climbing frame, that looked like a giant red spider… Stampy, Mathews, Moley and about ten other skinheads came out of nowhere, steamed in hard, broke little Sam's arm, Mucus had to take him up to A&E."

I felt sick, dropped the spliff into the ashtray, the smoke drawing an S shape in the air above it.

"Jesus Christ, the fucking bastards… I thought Stampy lived in Watton at Stone."

Whiff rocked forward on the bed, making it creak under his shifting weight, "He did, but after Duggan got shot, his family had to move for their own safety, I heard."

"So, the cunt's in Harlow, is he?"

"It looks like it: he's running with the Harlow Skinheads now."

"What's the name of that estate? Faircroft?" I started but trailed off as my bedroom door flew open.

In marched the old man, his brow furrowed. He wasn't messing around now; the phony war was over. It was time, time for the rapture. He sat down on the bed next to me, asked Whiff straight out if he had been involved with the booze blag. Oh fucking hell, I thought, why now? You could have said something to me last night,

131

this morning, why ask my mates? Why take it out on my mates? I shook my head, cringing at the intended accusation and hoped Whiff wasn't in the mood for one of his 'I didn't mean that either' jokes. Whiff could be volatile when adults started pestering him, giving him any bullshit, especially if he believed, or hadn't actually done anything wrong. I need not have worried though, the spliff had done its job.

Whiff calmly shook his head, holding the probing, furrowed glare. "No... It was nothing to do with me, I was in the Brewery Tap in Ware that night... I'm not into that sort of thing anyway, Mr. Baker," he said, glancing at me, eyes twinkling.

"Oh well, that's good to hear, some people find that sort of thing acceptable, why? God only knows, they don't value other people's property, do they? They will end up in jail and once they are inside, they'll realise that they are not as tough as they think they are... Mr. Big will rape them if they drop the soap in the showers."

Whiff snorted at the thought of it and the old man's focus homed in on the derision. "It's a fact, it's not a joke," he replied, closing Whiff down.

"People need to find a career, value hard work and effort, find their place in society, it's all there for anyone with a bit of gumption, all you need to do is......"

On and on he went, soon we both began to realise he wasn't really talking to Whiff at all; it was all for me, this was for my benefit, for my ears only. It didn't sound good, like it was the beginning of something new, maybe the end of something else. Something I had enjoyed since I had left school, a new direction which I was going to have march in, like it, or lump it.

In amongst it all, this barrage, this possible new order, something else became apparent. The old man was done with parenting; Frank Baker had had enough. He had two sons, my older brother Martin and me, and both of us had gone off the rails, as far as he was concerned. Martin, after a promising start, had fallen in with the wrong crowd at his comprehensive school - a comprehensive school system The old man had named, 'The Shirley Williams shit show, mediocrity for the masses'. Martin was totally out of control, had been expelled twice; the local authority didn't know what to do with him, and with all the other schools in the area refusing to take him, the school he had first been expelled from had to take him back for the fifth year, his last and probably most painful year at school for his teachers.

Once school was out, not just for summer, but forever, he became part of the early headhunters fighting out of the shed in Chelsea, to finance his trips to Chelsea and beyond on away days, where violence was never far away, he took a job panel beating in a local garage. In the end, he got so bad that the old man had bribed him with a second-hand Capri gear, and full tank of leaded to join the RAF, to get him back on the straight and narrow.

Martin wasn't into politics, but I was, so there was no way I was going into the armed forces, so what was he to do? He had completed his long service to society- forty years a Pay-As-You-Earn-Slave - he was retired now; his work was done as far as he was concerned. Frank Baker wanted to do things for himself, enjoy the time he had left, and being a parent just wasn't one of them. Of course, I was his son, I would be forever, but the day-to-day troubles that I found myself in from now on, would be my problems, my problems alone, not his anymore.

"If people want to throw their lives away it's up to them, why should I worry, I've done my bit, now it's time for others to take over, do their bit and if they don't, don't come crying to me, it's not my......"

I watched him as his mouth moved mechanically, masticating the vowels, crunching the consonants, eyes blazing with righteous indignation, putting the world in its place, when I noticed the smoke from the spliff in the ashtray next to the bed snaking its way up towards him.

Oh shit, I thought, willing it away and seeing that it wasn't responding to my will, I silently blew out of the corner of my mouth, trying to redirect the cobra-like plume. It was a waste of time. I watched in horror, grimacing as it slowly coiled its way around the old man's neck, snake-like, sought out his nose and promptly disappeared up one of his nostrils. A series of hacking coughs brought the old man's diatribe to a stuttering halt, he cleared this throat loudly. Once, twice, three times, all to no avail. Whatever had found its way inside him didn't agree with him. He shook his head, hoping to shake it off, all to no avail again. Baffled, he had completely lost his train of thought, then with a perplexed look on his face, he got up off the bed, silently walked out, and as the door clicked shut behind him, Whiff and me fell into fits of laugher.

"I'm sorry about that mate," I said through tears of laughter, "I knew it was coming, I don't know why he had to do that while you were here, it's the way he is sometimes, it's the scatter shot approach, he probably thinks he's helped you too."

"Oh don't worry about it, my old man's worse than yours, at least yours has a laugh sometimes, every time my old man opens his mouth, he just bores everyone to death." Whiff picked up the smouldering spliff, "I've got some good news; you're going to love this."

"Oh yeah, I reckon I'm due a bit of good news, what is it Whiff?"

"We've got a gig at Ware College, it's part of a week of concerts for the new intake of students."

"Oh what!? That's brilliant mate," I enthused, snatching the spliff from him, "I'll toke to that, that's great news."

I took a big pull, blowing it out like a Victorian steam engine. "How did you manage that?" I asked, handing it back to him.

"Mark Harper knows someone who works in the admin office at the college, so he gave them Andy's phone number… It's going to be a good one, him and his mates will be there, all the Ware lot should be coming along, you know Harper, don't you?" Asked Whiff, through a nimbus cloud of smoke.

I nodded, "I know Mark, he's a good bloke… For a skinhead that is, I did a bit of work with him for manpower services a while back, you know, the old Tory cheap labour racket, how do you know him?"

Whiff picked up his bass, hit a couple of strings, hinting it was time to practice, "I met him on the train going up to see The Exploited, you know the gig they played with Crass, the one where most of the skinheads spent the night zieg heiling? He wasn't into it at all, him and his mate Steve Bartlett, stood with the punks all night, he hates the NF, hates politics, especially right-wing ones."

I picked up my guitar, taking the hint plugged it in, thinking it would be good to see Mark again, while throwing a couple of chords onto the frets. Not only was he a good laugh, liked the same music that I did. He loved a drink and knowing that the student bar at the college was subsidised, I had a good idea how that night would turn out. It would be mayhem.

Whiff and me spent the rest of the afternoon going through the new track 'Spoils of War', puffing away between breaks in the practise, until the evening gently introduced itself by darkening the corners of my bedroom. I felt satisfied with our afternoons work and not just a little stoned, so we called it a day.

"I've been working on some new stuff, it's a bit of a different direction, you want a tape of it?" I asked as he was getting up to leave.

"Yeah, yeah, definitely, what is it?" Whiff said.

I smiled through my cotton mouth. "Virus V1 does Duran Duran," I joked. "Nah it's a bit darker than that, I'm calling it The Horror Tapes," I said as we walked downstairs,

"I've got loads of Virus V1 tracks ready to go, so I thought I would try writing something new, something really nasty, it's kind of like a video nasty punk."

"Sounds good Skin."

"I borrowed Basher's fuzz box, wrote a whole load of grinding slow riffs, overdubbed them with some semi-melodic haunting melodies, using the old tape to tape method for that extra low-fi sound."

Whiff nodded, keeping his eyes fixed on our narrow staircase.

"No politics in the lyrics either, just well...... Well, macabre stories of post-apocalyptic nightmares on a desolate, scorched planet, I suppose you could call it. It's still punk, but it's like a new station of punk."

Whiff laughed, "Upbeat, is it?"

I creased up, "Sorry Whiff, I don't know what I'm going on about, I think I might be a little bit stoned."

"Yeah, me too," said Whiff, stumbling forward, missing a step.

"Cheers for this Skin, I'll check them out later... With the sensi," he said, pocketing the tape along with the couple of spliffs I had given him earlier.

On my doorstep I asked, "What are you up to tonight? Are you and Andy going somewhere?"

Whiff snorted, "No way... You are joking, I'm not going out with him. No chance."

I scrutinized him, waiting for an explanation for this vitriol - they took the piss out of each other all the time, but this was something else. It was well over the top.

Whiff smiled. "Nah… He's alright… I haven't been out with Andy for ages… I don't see him much outside of the band these days," trying to make light of it.

I was stunned, totally taken aback. While I was hanging out with Dave in the village, I thought they would be hanging out in Ware together, either down The Tap or in the park, pissing off families with Whiff's boom box - they certainly used to.

"OK mate… Er…" I said, still slightly lost for words, "I'll see you at practice then, right, yeah, hope you enjoy the tape, it's fucking blinding mate… And the sensi."

Whiff punched his fist in the air, "Sensi!" Grinning from ear to ear. "Cheers Skin: I'll see you later," he said, disappearing into the rapidly-approaching darkness.

'I'm not hanging around with him, no chance' I thought, what's that all about? Andy and Whiff were mates long before I knew Whiff, ah, maybe he's stoned. In fact, if he's as stoned as I am, he could come out with anything, 'macabre stories of post-apocalyptic nightmares on a desolate, scorched planet' Jesus, did I really say that? What a pretentious wanker. I smiled to my pretentious wanker self, shut the door and behind me, the kitchen door edged open. It was mum, her face drawn, anguished, she pulled a tight smile onto her face, and beckoned me into the kitchen. Oh no what is it now? I can't be bothered, I thought, staring right back at her.

Mum whispered, "Mike come in here."

I stood smirking at her.

"Now," she said, more insistently.

I rolled my eyes, acquiescing, joined her in the kitchen. She
shut the door secretively behind us.

"Dad says you've got to get a job," she told me in a hushed tone.

I wasn't in the mood, particularly now, "Yeah, yeah."

"Mike listen, he says you've got to get a job, or we are
moving," almost pleading now.

I repeated, "Yeah, yeah, yeah," dismissing her
completely, opening the door to leave.

"And stop smoking that marijuana in your bedroom," She chided.

I paused by the door for a second, suppressed a laugh, shook my
head and strolled back off to the sanctuary of my bedroom.

Oh no, not this shit again, I thought, as I sat down on my bed. I
didn't want, or need a full-time job, all I wanted to do was write
music, play music, be part of the punk scene. It was going well too,
every day I was getting better on my guitar, my songwriting was
improving and after playing a couple of decent gigs at The Triad and
Bowes, we possibly, had our biggest gig so far, coming up at Ware
college. I didn't have time for a full-time job now. A full-time job
would be a massive distraction, it would take me away from what we
had achieved so far, and put me in that mouse race downward spiral
of work, sleep, work, sleep, work, sleep, repeat; fuck that for a laugh.
A whole lifetime term could be served on the dawn till dusk hamster
wheel, running for a carrot that was constantly plucked away by

greedy capitalist bosses, just so they could buy themselves yachts, cars, houses, and a million other things they felt they needed to own, to make themselves feel happy and relevant. If that wasn't bad enough, apart from Alan, all the bosses who I had to dealt with so far had been complete wankers. Dickhead autocrats, who thought they knew everything. Gesticulating, pontificating, telling me about the world - it was like, as I worked for them, they thought they owned me - they didn't. Nobody tells me what to fucking do, they could all fuck off as far as I was concerned. I had no respect for them. It was simple, when it came down to it; the bottom line was, I didn't like people telling me what to do, no matter how much or little I was paid, as my full-time employment record since leaving school would testify.

In the time since I had left school, it had been patchy to say the least. It had started badly in the blood, shit and stench of Patterson's farm in High Cross and ended pretty soon afterwards at Ron's shoe emporium in Hertford, with some silly old bastard having a heart attack over a few odor-eaters. I had a quick underpaid flirtation with AD and then, thankfully, the old man's Stalin-esque nagging about 'people who don't work, don't eat' had ceased. I had been left to my own devices, and the band had come on in leaps and bounds. It had been a productive time, I had written plenty of material, we had got underway, made a lot of progress, started getting a name for ourselves around Hertford and Ware, then a setback.

Once I had been out of work for a year, coming and going as I pleased, I received my first qualification ever. I was now classed as long term unemployed and had qualified to either work for the Man Power Services or go on a Y.O.P. or Youth Opportunities Program, as it was laughably called. Y.O.P was no opportunity for the youth whatsoever, it was an opportunity for bosses to get themselves some cheap labour; get workers to do the jobs that nobody else wanted to do, and did these young workers get a proper job with the company, as they were promised at the end of their program – did they bollocks, the companies just got more Y.O.P kids in.

I had no choice, I was qualified. It was either that or lose my Sosh money, so I plumped for the lesser of two evils, The Man Power services. I signed up on an archaeological dig in Ware, where I met Mark Harper and Steve Bartlett, which surprise, surprise, I enjoyed immensely. It wasn't to last, though; unfortunately, due to Tory cuts it didn't last the year that I signed up for and within a couple of months I was back to square one where gainful employment was concerned.

In the preceding year, I had found the perfect balance between getting enough money and having enough time for my music. A few times a week, depending on the season, I did some gardening work for Mrs. Gruber, a rich German widow, who for the most part was more interested in chatting rather than getting her garden done. Mrs. Gruber, or Alice as she liked to be called, paid me five pounds an hour for our impromptu conversations, which was a lot more than the average rate for an unskilled labourer. I carried on signing on too, which meant I usually ended up with more cash in my back pocket at the end of the week than most of my full-time working mates did. It was not only more than enough money for me, it was hilarious when you sat down and thought about it. There they were slogging their guts out for some wanker, to make him a millionaire, meanwhile, I was doing my own thing, writing music, having a few pints, enjoying life and as for the morality of it all; do they owe us a living? Of course, they fucking do.

I went to bed that night, thought it all through again, the one thing I was certain of was I wasn't going anywhere, as firstly it would be the end of the band and secondly, I had lived here all of my life, all my mates lived around here and although it was elementary now and Cerys was long gone, I didn't want to move away from her either. If mum and the old man did go, so what? I would go out and get a job. I enjoyed being a roof tiler - gardening or landscaping would be good too. In fact, I would do anything that I didn't have to think too much about anything that didn't take my mind away from the main thing in my life. Music. I could get my own place, rent a room somewhere and then there would be no more breaking into derelict houses or walking out into the countryside with my girlfriends, we could get really comfortable, stretch out, have some real fun. I could have my mates around at any time of the day or night, we could jam, have parties, have proper sessions. It could be the freedom I've been looking for; it could be brilliant. I don't need them, or this house, it's not my house anyway. If they want me to be independent, OK, so be it, I will be independent, and I'll be doing it away from them and their constant, paranoid nagging.

I mean, a backup plan??? Bollocks!!! Begging on the streets of London??? Bollocks, what are they on about!? I rolled over, getting comfortable, feeling the warmth building up, and my mum's scandalized words of 'And stop smoking that marijuana in your room', came back to me. I laughed to myself, slowly drifted off into a peaceful sleep.

Chapter 8

Mr. Laughter

In a not-so-far off place, Clare pulled me close, drawing me in, embracing me in her arms, around us the radiant orange richness of the street lights.

"I love it here Skinner, we could live here, it could be our home…"

"Aww, we could call it Deacon Towers," she told me, her voice full of the fun and laughter of someone young, carefree, unburdened by the complexities of life.

"Nah let's call it breast villas," I said, cupping her more than a handful boobs.

Clare laughed, "You are obsessed, you are."

"I am, with you Clare," I said gently moving in, docking my lips with hers.

"Hmmm," she said.

"Hmm" I returned.

Clare suddenly pulled away, fear scratching the surface of her face, "What the hell's that sound… It's footsteps, sodding hell, someone's coming, what are we going to do?"

I looked past her boggling eyes through the orange glow to see my old man pulling back my curtains, with one sweep he obliterated the orange glow and let the piercing sunlight flood into my bedroom.

"Jesus Christ, Dad!" I said, pulling my eiderdown around my waist, trying to cover up my pan handle like hard on. It was all to no avail though, so I rolled over, bending it painfully, flattening it into my divan.

"What time is it?" I whined.

"It's seven o'clock, now get up out of that stinky flea pit, you're getting a job today."

"Oh what, leave it out Dad."

"If you've got time to cause trouble, rob people, and all the other villainous little things you've been getting up to, then you've got too much time, the devil finds work for idle hands."

"I'm not idle, I'm a guitarist, I'm in a band… And we've got a big bloody gig coming up," I shouted at his retreating back as he left me to reassemble.

"And you'll still be in a band after you get a job, or is it a punk prerequisite that only unemployed layabouts can join?" I heard him laugh as he thumped back downstairs.

Oh shit, twice oh shit, I thought.

One, oh shit, for the fact that he hasn't given up on me yet. Why hasn't he given up on me? 'It's not my problem', he said. 'It's your problem', he said, so OK, let it be my problem, just give up on me, move if you're going to. Sod off. I'll do what I need to do when the time comes.

144

Oh shit, number two, he was actually happy to be helping me out, which really was daunting, as the last time he had helped me out it had turned into a total head fuck.
I can't believe this. It won't last, surely, it's only a stay of execution.

I smiled to myself, thinking that this morning's positive old man, with his brand-new fairy-liquid shiny demure, coupled with his anti-corporal punishment stance wouldn't last once he saw what his beloved Tories had done to the job market. In fact, the way those bastards were going, it wouldn't be long before all the birds and the bees would be unemployed, too, languishing on the dole. I smirked, rolled back over, trying to conjure up the dream I was having. Clare was long gone though, my dick was dead, my smirk died; reality it was then. I pulled back my eiderdown, chucked it onto the floor, my feet following, and as I landed this small step, I felt the breadcrumbs from yesterday's snack in the thread-bare carpet. Bollocks I thought, grinding them in, out of sight. Then I grabbed my clothes, threw them on, went downstairs, had a quick breakfast and after an even quicker wash, and we set off for the Ware Job Centre.

On the way down the A10, I braced myself for some kind of lecture, maybe something in the vein of what he had said to me via Whiff in my bedroom yesterday, before Mary Jane had thrown him; addled his bald pate. I heard nothing from him, though. No pep talk, no call to arms, no, who was right, who was wrong, no good, no bad, no heaven, no hell. The oceans of the world, the stars above, and everything else in between were his specialist subjects. There seemed to be no end to his knowledge, or so he thought. Sometimes when it seemed like the verbal assault would never end, I would drift off into a world of music, zoning out, stop being crushed by the unassailable weight of words, and the twisted logic accompanying them.

On some occasions it was impossible to escape the avalanche of
knowledge that was falling onto my aching bonce, so I would have
to listen. It was funny sometimes, as he would try to wing it, lecture
me on things that he knew absolutely nothing about. So I would quiz
him, ask him questions as my bullshit detector engaged, catch him
out, and he'd smile, nodding sagely like he'd taught me something. I
heard nothing today though, none of it; he just kept his eyes on the
road, coaxing our mustard-coloured Mini 850cc up the hills and
around the bends.

In his mind, the time for talking was over; it was now time for
action. I sat back, enjoying the unusual silence, watching the world
waking up, yawning, stretching itself, readying itself. The sun glowing
in the east throwing out its first tentative rays of the new day, the
clouds marching in from the west in the prevailing winds. In
amongst it all, all this beauty, was the traffic, the drones inside their
metal boxes, arduously making their way to work. A hundred cars all
going in the same direction; nowhere and boredom, their occupants,
all doing their bit for society, giving, giving, giving on a daily basis,
while some rich bastard could keep on taking, taking, taking.

I started writing lyrics in my head.

Rush for an hour, you'll never get back again,
Why are you rushing? fuck the boss, get in at ten.
You keep on rushing, you're a slave,
Your life's over, rushing to your grave.

I thought, I've got a couple of decent medium pace riffs ready to go
with it, it needs a bit of work, but it's a strong start. To nowhere and
beyond, would be its title until I found something better. Glancing at
the old man, I saw that he was miles away too, probably thinking
about Esther Rantzen again, I thought, laughing to myself.

I wondered what he was really thinking about, he was sixty years old, retired now, did he dream? Did he still have dreams? Have places he wanted to visit? Things he wanted to do? In fact, did he still actually want to do anything? I remembered when he was at work, he didn't; he spent his time reading the newspaper, watching the news, winding himself up, hating how the world was going. It was like he was so drained after work; he just couldn't help himself; it was easier for him to be negative than positive. He was drawn to it, like flies to shit. It really was strange him not talking, giving me some advice, his silence was unnerving; maybe it was meant to be.

A while later, the old man was parking up the car in the car park behind Ware college. I thought about our up-and-coming gig here, but I was quickly pulled back to reality.

"OK, so where's the Job Centre?" The old man asked.

"It's over there, right next to the college… The perfect place for it," I grinned.

"Let's go," The old man huffed, totally ignoring the intended joke.

I showed him the all-too-familiar route to 'The No Job Centre' as it was known by the people who used it, the people who knew, and opening the door, he followed me into the airless, stale environment, where we split up, like victims in a horror film, to see what we could find.

I wandered through the dozen or so boards, peering at the little yellow cards with the jobs written on them. I counted twelve, which was about the average number for Ware Job Centre. It was always the same: a complete waste of time, if it wasn't for the fact that you had to be seen to be actively searching for employment to get the Sosh Giro bonanza, the place would have fewer visitors than Peter Sutcliffe.

On the last board I came to, the one that usually held the worst of the meagre bunch. I saw with mounting horror an ad for a toilet attendant in Ware, I quickly ripped it from the board, crushing it, slipping it into my pocket, hiding it from prying eyes. Jesus fucking Christ, I thought, a fucking toilet attendant! Prospects to go straight to the bottom of the U-bend.

"You see anything Mike?" said, the old man sidling up next to me.

"No there's nothing,"

"I tell you this country has gone down the toilet,"

I stifled a laugh, sighed, "Yeah… It's no good Dad, most of these jobs need a driving licence."

"Oh, now wait just a minute, what about these?" He asked, drifting off in the direction of the office jobs.

"I'm not qualified to work in an office… Da … You need O levels."

"Not for this you don't," he said, his head thrusting forward like a Heron spearing its prey, and in one fell swoop off the board it came, "Here's one, it's in printing."

"I'm not interested in printing, Dad, I want to work outside."

"Oh, don't worry about that, this is better," he said, waving me away confidently, grinning like he'd found the final solution to all of our problems, "It's an apprenticeship, which means the pay starts off low while you train, then once you qualify you can make a lot of money, you can move between different jobs, the companies will be looking for you rather than you going to them, you can choose who you work for, you'll be your own boss, you could have your own business by the time you are forty, come on let's see if we can get you an interview."

Oh well, I thought, he didn't stay silent for long, did he? He must have been storing it all up for the big push, where did our uncompanionable silence go? I was enjoying that. I didn't know what to say, or how to say it; it sounded like a bloody nightmare, a twenty-year bloody nightmare at that, but he was on a mission this morning, and as far as he was concerned, there was no way I was leaving here without at least getting an interview.

"Er... OK Dad, I'll give it a go," I said, knowing full well that getting an interview and actually getting the job were two totally different things.

I was probably due an interview anyway, the Sosh bonanza could be removed at any time if the city drones at D.H.S.S thought the claimant was not getting on his bike every morning, searching, searching, always searching. So that was it, it was out of my Giro grabbing hands;
between the old man and 'your benefits have been cut off letter', the decision had been made for me. My interview was set
for three o'clock that afternoon at the printer's company in Hertford and as far as the old man was concerned, my future was secured.

In the car on the way back, the old man was telling me all about printing, surprise, surprise, he knew everything there was to know about printing. He had never done it before, but he knew alright, after a while I stopped listening, dropped the portcullis, started thinking about what I was going to do this afternoon, about getting the bus again. I hadn't been on a bus since school, these days if I wanted to go to Ware, I would either walk or if Dave was about, he would drive me down. I didn't want to take the piss though, so I would usually end up walking, sitting here now I saw an opportunity to rectify that though, and stop the word tsunami too.

"I think I need to get my driving licence, Dad," I interrupted, breaking through the wall of words.

"Yes, yes, that's a good idea, Mike," he nodded enthusiastically, pleased that I was actually looking to achieve 'something real'.

"Oh yes driving... I've been driving for forty years," he became even more animated now he actually knew what he was talking about.

I nodded back, "It would get me about, I could..."

"Forty years I've been driving..." he cut across me.

A whole five minutes passed in an hour as he told me how he had learned to drive, some of the dos and don'ts that he had picked up in his 'forty-odd years of road use' and on and on and on it went. It began to feel like my brain was melting, dribbling down my back onto the seat, so I dropped the portcullis again, all to no avail this time. I was drowning under a tidal wave of words, oxygen starved I zoned out and watched the trees zip past the window, occasionally nodding my head, saying, 'oh yeah' and 'that's right'.

Into the house we walked, and he was still dribbling on, and I was still nodding my head mechanically, mum smiled, happy in the knowledge that we were communicating again, had something in common to talk about, even though she could see it was all one-way traffic. In fact, it was total gridlock, a traffic jam, a slow escalating incident that I had to escape from. So I made my getaway, fleeing the sonic barrage, driving myself away, off to my bedroom, telling them I needed to smarten myself up for the interview at Ashwell Printers.

"That's a good idea, Mike," followed me upstairs.

Once I had reached the sanctum, I sat down, looked at my range of clothes. I only had bondage trousers, and grinned at the thought of turning up at Ashwell Printers wearing my favoured yellow tartan pair, complete with bondage straps and bum flap. The look on their faces would be priceless, not only that, 'The Ruperts' would secure the result I wanted. 'Get out punk' -perfect.

On the way out, I knew I would never get passed the old man wearing them though, so I picked out my Gringo black bondage trousers, which were the least punky looking ones I had, undid the straps, took the white tartan bum-flap off the backside. So far, so good. On the back of the legs of the trousers, there were a couple of long black zips, which I couldn't take off. I stopped in my tracks, thought it over. I could probably get out of the house without the old man noticing, if I turned to wave to him as I left, then later on at the interview no one would notice them until I left: The interview would be over long before that.

"You need to get your skates on, Mike," Mum warned from downstairs.

"It won't look good, if you turn up late," said the old man on my case too.

"It's fine, the bus doesn't leave till two, I've got plenty of time, they're usually late anyway," I said from my Mum's room, checking my trousers in her lonely, unused vanity mirror. 'Hmm… Lovely', it said, giving me the two thumbs up. So trousers sorted, I pulled on my white sleeping T-shirt, the without the holes in, or the upside-down effigy of the crucified Christ being pissed on by two cowboys, and checked the mirror again.

"Ha, ha, so who is the scruffiest oik of them all?" I asked it.

"Why you are, you scruffy bastard," my mirror image replied.

I stood, taking myself in, thinking, I'm a young go-getter, A yuppy, sarcastically, then I bared my teeth, growled, gave the mirror self the two-finger salute and padded off to the bathroom to scrub my face, shave and wash my hair; it wouldn't take long to finish off the masterpiece.

"Mike! You've got fifteen minutes to get to the bus stop, come on, hurry!" Shouted my Mum.

"Five minutes, Mike, move it!" Added the old man, distractedly.

Whiff had leant me his mum's hair clippers a few weeks earlier, so I had given myself a number two and died it blonde with peroxide; it had grown out a bit since then and was a decent length now, so that could be a problem. It looked almost normal. I gave it a quick spike-up with a bit of hair gel, just to make sure people knew where my heart lay, it didn't move.

One more glance in the mirror at the end product told me I was ready, then shouting a hasty goodbye to mum and the old man who thankfully were sitting in the living room, I swept out of the house and made my way up to catch the bus for the first time in years.

Once I had made it up to the bus stop, in plenty of time, as I knew I would do, some memories started coming back, that doomed feeling, the feeling of control, of contempt and compliance. I thought back to the cold and frosty mornings and the other kids faces; faces I had only seen the night before, that had been smiling, laughing, chatting, which were now silenced, downcast, dreading another day in full-time education and the bullshit that came with it. In the first couple of minutes of waiting, I began to get the bus stop tick too, an involuntary movement whereby my head swivelled automatically down the road, eyes searching to see if the bus was coming, it wasn't. A tick that also made me look into The Sow and Pig's pub window opposite the bus stop to see what the time was. It was ten past two, well surprise, surprise, the bus was late, and then I actually felt the silly worries about whether it was going to show up at all, all the while in the background, the gnarling feeling that I didn't want to get on the bloody thing anyway.

"Oi, you alright Skinner? Where you going?" Shouted Danny, breaking the monotony, strutting across the road towards me, a broad grin on his face.

"I've got a fucking job interview, haven't I?"

Danny gave me the once-over, looked confused. "Er... Skinner, your interview clothes are the same as your normal clothes," he said creasing up laughing.

"Well yeah... I don't want the fucking job, do I?"

"I see," Danny nodded sagely, like it was the most sensible thing he had heard all day.

I looked to see if the bus was coming, unsurprisingly it wasn't, so turning back to Danny, I rolled my eyes in frustration and saw his mouth flop open like a drawbridge.

"What's up with you? You look like you've seen a ghost," I asked.

Danny pointed wordlessly and there, quite clearly, was the light blue Panda car of Pigman Cannon trundling up the road towards us. I snorted, thinking this is too good to miss, so I stuck my thumb out like I was hitch-hiking. Danny quickly followed suit, then pulled up his trouser leg, flashing a bit of flesh to make picking us up even more enticing to The Tamworth. We both smiled broadly and watched Cannon's crumpled face snarling back at us as he passed us by.

"Wanker!" Shouted Danny, putting the icing on the cake.

Cannon's brake lights flashed an angry red, then almost at once, off again, and he hit the accelerator, and carried on, leaving Danny and me in stitches.

"See ya, cunts table," I said, waving sarcastically.

Danny eyed the trundling little Panda, "Did you see the look on his face?"

I nodded, watching too, "All that shit he caused us, the fucking bastard, that's why I'm here, wasting my precious time, going to a job interview for a job I don't want."

"I, er… Yeah, we all got it bad," he said, looking down into the tarmac.

"Lee and Glyn … Fucking hell." I said.

"Yeah…"

I could tell he had something on his mind, so I waited, knowing Danny he would get there eventually, he couldn't help himself; he thought, he spoke.

"So, Skinner… Have you seen Ronnie around?" Asked Danny, trying to sound casual - Danny couldn't do casual in a Pringle top and Chinos.

I said, "No, why have you?" Cagily.

Danny laughed, "No.. No one has since the booze blag, he hasn't been out since then."

"It's been a while now, hasn't it? Is he still shitting himself then?" I asked, glancing to the corner again for the missing bus. Nope, nothing.

Danny nodded sadly, "Yeah, he's been in a right
state," playing the sympathy card for his mate.

"I would have thought he would have shitted himself dry by now."

I thought, OK, he's testing the waters for him. "I don't know about
anyone else, but I won't touch him," I stated. "I doubt it anyway," I
added, laughing.

Danny smiled, satisfied in the knowledge that he had found out
where I stood on the matter, or at least he thought he did. The truth
was, I didn't know what my reaction would be when I bumped into
Ronnie, AKA Mr. T.U.R.D. again. A lot had happened to Dave and
me since the booze blag, Lee and Glyn too. I had seen the red welts
on their backs, heard their sad stories. It had been so much worse
for them; they'd had a proper clobbering.

One way or another it had been a bad experience for us all, if the
clampdown was over for Dave and me, and if I was in a good mood,
having a few drinks, back to enjoying life again, I'd probably leave it,
just have a word. If the clampdown continued or got even worse, I
was more likely to go with my first idea of what I was going to do to
him when I saw him; clamp my fucking D.Ms down onto his stupid
fucking grassing head.

Danny asked, "What are you doing later? I'm meeting up with
Ashley, we're probably going up to herb central." Putting his
business aside.

"I don't know, I'll probably be in The Anchor later celebrating not
getting this job."

Danny nodded thoughtfully.

"I haven't seen Ashley for a while, how is he these days? Is he still bullshitting?" I asked, scratching my smoothly shaved chin.

Danny laughed, "You know Ashley, he can't stop, I reckon he's got brown blood."

I creased up laughing, checked the corner again and hallelujah; miracles of miracles I saw the 331 from Buntingford to Hertford slowly nosing its way towards us. A moment later, it pulled up next to us, the doors hissing open.

"See you man, say hello to Ashley for me, tell him I'll see him soon," I said, hopping on.

Danny gave me a grin, a wave and wished me good luck in fucking it up. I told him I didn't need luck, I was a natural; a natural fuck-up, and assured him that I would still be unemployed at the end of the day. He laughed back, the doors hissed shut, and I was off to my first proper job interview in years. I had to grip the bars as I stamped along the bus, as the driver must have heard something he didn't like in me and Danny's conversation as I hopped on his bus, and as a consequence. He was now smashing the gears home, loosing off the clutch, making the bus pitch hideously, throwing me around with it. I thought ha, ha, wanker.

I sat back in my seat and watched the world as it slowly reeled past the window, the fields were a light brown hue, vast and showing the first signs of spring green. It was a new beginning, a new start, I thought, apart from the wanker at the helm, it wasn't so bad being back on the bus after all, especially at this time of the day when there were only a few of us onboard; it was certainly a lot less effort than walking. I started day-dreaming about an arch of orange light running smoothly across a beautiful white translucent body underneath me and wondered whether I would ever see that again. If my dreams came true, I would. What a dream, that was turning into this morning. Inwardly, I laughed at the old man's untimely intervention; it could have been a lot worse, I supposed. I was shaken, from my tangerine dreams as the hydraulic door hissed open once again, as the bus pulled up at its first stop in Ware.

A couple of old women got on, smiling, nodding, a hello at the bus driver, who gave them a rictus grin, took their money, chucked some change at them, shut the doors and hit the accelerator, before they could take their seats. One of the old dears nearly went down, throwing her walking stick out to balance herself. If it wasn't for her friend, who was slightly more robust than her, grabbing her arm she probably would have done.

Oh what, I thought, who is this twat? I edged over in my seat, checked his face in the long mirror in the front window and saw he was an old bloke in his mid-fifties, overweight, balding, his face red, angry his life fucked up. He wasn't going to nowhere or to boredom he was going to Hertford from Buntingford, no wonder he was pissed off, I would take nowhere and boredom any day. I began wondering, at what point in his life did he think: I want to be a bus driver; did he grow up thinking that? I imagined him when he was a kid, back at school in the playground, talking to his mates "No… I don't want to be a pilot like you Peter, or an astronaut like you Jonathan, or a soldier like you Albert, or a sailor or an actor or an artist… No, it's the bus driver's life for me, tra-la, la." I shook my head dismissively and thought fuck that, if that's the way it makes you feel, you should have set your sights on being something else. It would be like me taking this printer's job, sell my soul for a few quid: no chance, I'm going to live my life. My way.

On Ware High Street, it was the same as ever, we hit the usual heavy traffic, slowing us down to a crawl. I stretched back in my seat and watched the shops slowly pass the window. Saville's newsagent, Rumbelows, then out of Boots, the thief's paradise, stepped Stampy and Moley, followed by Karen Corker and Ski Sunday. I ducked down in my seat, hoping that I hadn't been spotted, but too late, Karen's face spilt into one of her beautiful smiles.

"Skinner, Skinner, you alright?" She shouted, running over, bringing me to the attention of the two big, Crombie wearing, Skinheads who stopped in their tracks, dossing me out.

I smiled at her, ignoring the menacing faces, "Hi Karen you alright?" I asked brazenly, focusing on her completely, filtering out the scum, and even though she had tried to use me, mess me up, trap me. I couldn't help myself. She was beautiful, great fun, but she was damaged, deadly, especially in this company, I still wanted to spend more time with her though.

"Where have you been? Have you been hiding from me?" She laughed.

"Nah course not, when you coming up the village next?"

On the window in between us, a clod of phlegm appeared. I heard laughter, pulled my eyes away from Karen's smiling face, saw the two Skinheads rocking backwards in their blood-red D.Ms, watching the soppy cunt on the bus. I felt angry, leant forwards, licking at the frothy saliva.

"Oh ha-ha, fuck off, wankers!" I shouted.

In a second, they were on the window slavering like mad dogs, they barked, threatened, pointed, slamming their fists onto the feeble glass. It shook, buckled, making me cringe away, and scaring the other passengers on the bus, who cowered forward, keeping low, keeping out of it, hoping they would go away. One look towards the bus driver told me he wasn't interested. It wasn't his problem, none of his business. His eyes were focused on the road ahead, then thankfully the road ahead opened up, the traffic moved off, and we pulled away, leaving the Crombie coated cunts doing cut-throat motions slicing at their necks with their hands.

"You're fucking dead, dead punk, dead," Stampy told me.

Karen stood behind them, open-mouthed, stunned, a little girl, a little girl lost, out of her depth, sinking fast. Next to her Ski Sunday leaned on her shoulder, laughing at the rabid dogs incessant yapping.

I was dead now, officially; my death certificate had been prepared; it had the cause of death: throat cut with a knife. It had two of the perpetrators, but knowing my luck, the next time I bumped into Stampy and Moley, the rest of the Wolf Pack would be there too, all it needed now was a date and an approximate time.

"Yeah, yeah, yeah, fuck off wankers, fucking wankers," I shouted, watching them disappearing in the diesel fumes of the bus, there was nothing to lose now.

I thought, why is she hanging out with them, she isn't even a Skinhead anymore? Why? It didn't make sense. Oh no, surely, she hasn't gone and got pregnant with one of them, has she? I knew she was desperate, wanted to get away from her drunk of a mum and her revolving door of boyfriends, but fucking hell, talk about jumping out of the frying pan into the fire.

Karen's future? It was no future: Stampy and Moley were animals, vicious bullies, loved inflicting pain, it was easy for them. I saw the future Karen, saw her battered face as the Skinheads' frustration with the world came to the surface in flashes of rage, saw the concern on the health workers faces as they visited the troubled household. The baby innocent, yet guilty of being born into a house that nobody really wanted it, and finally, the inevitable swoop by the social services, to take the baby away from the toxic environment that surrounded its birth mum.

Once we were out of Ware, the bus picked up speed and as it did, I watched the phlegm on the window pulling, thinning, then finally dissipating into the rushing air, and along with it went my fear. I settled back again, to watch the ever-repeating views. It looked different now, somehow, the mundane becoming comforting, re-assuring, even. The bus passed the Chadwell Springs golf course, where Dave had got his one in hole, courtesy of Jill. The job where Dave and me had dug the trench that had turned into a dance school for wheelbarrows, and a good caking for anyone who walked past, then finally, probably the best of all was that the post office run by the Pakistani family; their windows were not boarded up; it was glass all the way.

A few stops later, I alighted at the bus station in the centre of Hertford, giving the driver a pitying look as I marched past him. He didn't care he was too busy scowling at the world through his caustic window to be bothered with what I was doing. I reasoned why would he? He was living in his self-made personal hell every day; he's seen it all before.

I wandered up Fore Street, passed Gays the newsagent, a place that was always worth a joke in the first year at Richard Hole, good for the odd free chocolate bar too - that is until they brought in the five kids only in the shop at one time rule - which made pilfering a lot more difficult. On past The White heart pub I trudged, then I looked through the railings of the underpass and there it was, horror of horrors. Richard Hole, still standing, still producing boring, stifled characterless robots for the City of London to use in its quest to rob the poor of the world.

Into Parliament Square I walked past The Blackbirds pub, and up onto the industrial estate off Gascoigne Way, where Ashwell Printers loomed large in front of me. I felt a bit of deja vu, it looked like one of the corrugated iron hen houses at High Farm, my first job. It entered my mind to piss off, leave it, go and have a pint in the Black Horse pub on West Street. It couldn't be though, I would never get away with it, the old man and the Sosh would be all over me quicker than Stampy and Moley. I pushed on the door, hoping it might be locked, it wasn't, it flew open, there was no turning back now, I trudged into the small, hutch like reception area.

"Oh hello, are do fir ultimate view this moon?" The middle-aged woman in milk bottle glasses, seemed to say from behind her desk in reception.

I couldn't hear a thing, the racket coming from inside, from what I presumed was the printing room, was incredible. It shook everything, the walls, the furniture, the floor beneath me was positively dancing, had my almost, covered-up D.M.s doing the moon dance.

"WHAT?" I asked, cupping my ear.

A knowing look passed over her face.

"I'M SO SORRY!" She shouted, jumping up to shut the door that led, into the belly of the place. Once the heavy fire door was closed, she said,

"Aaaahhh yes that's better, I'm so sorry about that, it can get very noisy in here during a print run. I'm used to it now, probably a bit deaf, are you one of the interviewees for this afternoon?"

"Yeah, one of them," I said, smiling to myself.

"And your name please?"

"I'm Baker, Michael Baker."

"Michael… Baker," she repeated as she wrote it down, "You are early, you must be keen, take a seat please."

"Oh yeah very much so, it's been a dream of mine for years."

"Wonderful, wonderful, that's wonderful," she said, totally missing my sarcasm.

I exhaled thoroughly, thinking those fucking buses have let me down again, I should have had that pint after all. Bored already I had a look around.

In front of me, a small, blackened window gave view into the noisy print room floor, I saw how enclosed and prison-like it was. In amongst the machines, boiler-suited inmates ghosted backwards and forwards, serving their machines obediently, silently. It was then that the stark reality of the situation I was in really hit me. If I was unlucky enough to get this job, I will be spending eight hours a day in this non-environment, possibly for years, then just like the bus driver earlier. It would be me with the sour look on my face, forever living in a world that I hated. I thought, whatever I do, I must not get this job; it was time to use all the skills I had learned over the years; time to fuck it up beyond all recognition.

A couple more boiler-suited drones joined the others on the print room floor, and began feeding the machines with ink and paper. The machines thirstily drank the ink, clawed the paper, pulling it, pasting it, passing it through its bowels, then belched it out of the side in high definition.

"Miidjh d ddj!"

"Sjsj dddhd fdjdff!"

"WHAT!?"

"OH SORRY!" She said, thumping the door home again, "Alec will see you now, go on in."

OK I thought, it's time, time to end this waste of time. I smirked, stood up, pulled up my trousers, revealing my half laced up, black sixteen-hole D.M.s.

"In through there, that's it, in front of you, just follow the sound of the printers."

I threw a wry smile at the secretary, pushed open the door with Interview Room written on it as hard as I could, and entered. Alec the interviewer's first impression, the one I couldn't repeat, said 'OUT'. I was halfway there already. All I needed to do now was show I couldn't give a shit.

Alec knew it was a long process, a process that must be done by the book, so re-adjusting his face, setting it to neutral he said, "Hello, I'm Alec Slaughter," indicating for me to be seated.

"Ha, I know, yes, I saw the look on your face, I've seen it many a time before, it's not a nice name, is it?" He said in his rehearsed opening, like it was totally off the cuff.

"What, Alec?" I replied, warming up, getting into my stride.

Alec stopped in his tracks, he was off-piste now, he floundered for a second. "Oh, yes, good one, yes, well, we like a sense of humour here, you don't have to be mad to work here, but it helps," he said getting back on script again, "No, I don't like my name, Slaughter, so I take the S off, so it's actually Laughter, Laughter, which is what we like the sound of around here. OK so let's talk about something more interesting, you, how…"

On cue, a huge, mechanized blast of seismic proportions ripped through the factory, drowning him out. I couldn't hear a word he was saying, but by his hand gestures I saw he had asked me something. It could have been, 'What's the capital of Poland?' for all I knew as the noise from the printers engulfed everything around us, so I gestured for him to repeat it.

Mr. Laughter smiled patiently, watching carefully how the interviewee reacted under pressure, and repeated the question a little louder this time, and once again, for me, it was lost in the churning racket of the print room floor.

I thought it would have been embarrassing for the both of us to ask him to repeat the question for the third time, so I smiled inanely and said, "Warsaw."

Mr. Laughter pulled a puzzled face, shrugged minutely, crooked his neck, scribbled something on the blank piece of paper in front of him, and carried on, his mouth working overtime.

I thought I heard the words 'pint ran over' and then like magic 'the print run was over' and it became very quiet in the office,

Mr. Laughter smiled magnanimously, rubbing his hands together, and now we could actually hear each other, the interview properly began in earnest...

"OK right Michael, we've got all the clerical bumf here, you are eighteen, you attended Richard Hale school, excellent, excellent. I'm an old boy myself, hmm, not much of a work history, but well that's OK, probably just haven't found the job for you, or your niche, as I would say, let's cut to the chase, get to the meat and gravy of The Printer Michael Baker," he chuckled to himself. "Why are you interested in working in the printing industry?" He asked.

Inside I felt a quiver, it was the perfect start for me, the old man had asked me exactly the same thing last night, in a mock interview. I had repeated parrot fashion, 'I've always been interested in publishing, taking pictures, I read the newspapers every day'. In my bedroom later on, I had made up my own mind on what I was going to say for this starter for ten.

"I used to do a paper round," I smiled broadly.

Mr. Laughter looked at me for a while like there was a punch line coming, it wasn't coming. I didn't have one. I just sat there looking back at him evenly, and he scribbled something down.

Strike one.

"Why do you want this job, Michael?"

I shot back, "I need a job,"

"Oh yes, yes, well... Everyone needs a job, ha, ha, yes," he replied, titling his head from side to side, like he was weighing it up in his head.

Strike two. His pen slicing across the paper.

"OK, OK, OK, right and finally where do you see yourself in ten years?"

"Oh, I don't know... I haven't got any long-term plans mate."

I thought, yep, that should do it.

Strike three!!!

I thought that would be it, it would be the end of it, this waste of time and I would be released to go and do something much less boring instead. I was very much mistaken, though. Mr. Laughter was a man of procedure, a man of crossed T's and dotted I's. A man who was probably trying to run the clock down himself, so he carried on for another fifteen minutes, telling me what my duties would be, he even talked about holiday pay. It was pure farce, I was sitting there, trying to persuade someone that I was interested in a job that I wasn't interested in, and he in turn was sitting there, looking back at me, trying to pretend that the job was available to me, even though he knew that I wasn't interested in it, and he wasn't going to give it to me anyway.

In the end, a smiling Mr. Laughter limply shook my hand, and told me they would write and let me know what we both already knew. I would never work for Ashwell Printers.

Oh thank fuck for that, I thought. It was like all of my worst nightmares rolled up in one, I couldn't wait to get out of there. I would have essentially been a cog in a machine, a machine that coloured paper while discolouring human beings. In a hurry now, I threw the door open, took a breath of the fresh air, and left the ear-rupturing noise of the machines behind me for some other poor bastard. I pounded back to the bus station, and as bad luck would have it, the very same miserable bus driver took my money and chucked another ticket in my direction.

I sat down, scrutinizing him as he scowled at the world through his corrosive window, something had changed in me, something in the interview, the farce at the end, maybe he didn't want this job either, maybe he hadn't dreamt about being a bus driver after all, maybe he wanted to be something else, couldn't do it, had other pressures on him. In his youth he had no choice, buckled under the weight of responsibility, financial, family, hand-to-mouth dependents relying

on him to make it through the week. I should respect the bloke, he's
a provider, a grafter. I didn't know how long he had been driving
buses, but maybe his old man had insisted that he should get a job,
any old job when he left school and here, he was, thirty-odd years
down the line, still doing it, and hating every minute of it, but still
doing it all the same. I started feeling guilty. It was a sobering
thought, and even though his bloodshot, hate-filled eyes paused,
boring in on me as he edged out into the evening rush-hour traffic, I
began to feel some sympathy for the miserable old sod. It was a sad
indictment of the, some win, some lose, society that we lived in.
A society where people had to endure all kinds of tedium just to
keep their heads above the water to pay their bills. It made me even
more determined to live my life the way I wanted too, and not
for the first time that day I thought... Whatever it takes.

A thoughtful bus ride later, we pulled up at the Sow and Pigs bus
stop back in Thundridge, and now I understood the man
better, I gave him a friendly nod as I got off.

"Cheers, mate," I said, cordially over my shoulder.

"Yeah, cheers, shitter."

"You what?" I asked, spinning around on him, his eyes didn't move,
he steadily watched the mass of traffic on the road ahead of him,
waiting to close the doors.

Cheers mate indeed, I thought, I didn't see you doing anything when
those wankers were kicking the shit out of your bus, you did fuck all,
sat there like a plum, pretending to watch the traffic. You knew
exactly what was going on and did nothing, then you hassle me?
Calling me a shitter? It's not really about me, though, is it? When it

comes down to it, it's about you. You not having the guts to change your miserable life. You're the shitter, mate. You need to look at yourself before passing your judgement on other people. If you don't like the bed you're lying in, then change it, do something about it, it's simple. In this society, the bottom line is, you either die on your feet, or live on your knees, or in your case, live in a chair for your whole life.

"You're a wanker mate," I told the side of his bald head, and strolled off his bus with my head held high, the mechanical hiss of the hydraulic doors putting an end to our exchange.

I watched him slowly edge the bus back out into the rush hour traffic and lumber off towards High Cross, while I strolled along the path, homeward-bound.

On the way back, I was so preoccupied with Karen, Stampy, Moley, my impending death at the hands of The Wolf Pack, the wanker bus driver, and Mr. Laughter, that I almost bumped into Lucy Harrington on the relief road at the side of my house. She looked great in her usual baggy top and jeans, slacker's outfit. I hadn't spoken to her since Tarnia Gorden's piss party, but ever the optimist, I thought I would see if she had forgiven me, or better still forgotten it.

I smiled, "You alright Lucy, how you going?"

. . .

"Lucy? You alright?" I asked, at her retreating figure.

. . .

"Oh what, what's up with you!? Whiff was only having a laugh."

"Oh yeah, big laugh Skinner, everyone drinking your piss all night, you dirty bastard."

"Oi, Oi, Oi, I stopped them from pissing in your drink!" I cried.

"Sod off you deviant, don't talk to me ever again."

I've had enough of this day I thought, so I careered off down the relief road and pounded back into the kitchen at my house, finding mum and the old man sitting down for tea. I hadn't even got my backside on the chair, when they started going on, excitedly asking me how it went. I told them I felt confident about the job, which was true, I did feel confident, confident that I wouldn't have to be cooped up in that shit hole for eternity and a day.

Chapter 9

Nice Legs Shame About the Boat Race

Whiff and me had been talking about making a demo tape to get us some more exposure, as the satellite world we lived in was small. Small and getting smaller as The Prime Munster, Maggie Thatcher's cuts took hold, putting people on the dole and sending the venues to the wall. One of Whiff's mates in Ware had a Fostex four-track that he reckoned he might be able to get hold of. Paranoid John, his mate, was careful with it though, like he was with everything, but being a fellow smoker, Whiff told me a little baggy from herb central would do nicely for him.

Ashley hadn't been seen in the village for a long time. I assumed he was ducking and diving, fucking and skiving as ever, so there would be no baggy coming from his direction - not until whatever scam he was involved in finished, anyway. On many occasions, Danny and me had talked about getting the train up to Dalston Junction and wandering over to Hackney Frontline, to get sorted. Danny had basically disappeared off the face of Thundridge, too, since I had seen him that day at the bus stop, when we had tried to thumb a lift, in 'my little panda' as we had renamed Cannon's bacon delivery wagon. So with no little baggy for four-track leverage, sadly, it would be awhile before we could make our demo, to get our name out there.

Once we did have our demo tape, we knew plenty of places to send it, as all of us had steadily been collecting contacts from the back of records, flyers, and the music papers, Sounds and the 'Enema' NME, over the years just for this very purpose. I had even managed to get Cal, the vocalist from Discharge's, phone number from Pooch, their new guitarist. I doubted it would be any use, though, as for a laugh, a pissed-up Whiff and me had given him a bell pretending to be the Kemp brothers from Spandau Ballet. I told had him we needed a vocalist, quickly, as Tony Radley was on his rag week, and Cal had told me to fuck off, before slamming the phone down.

In the meantime, for Virus V1, it was business as usual. It was all about the next gig, and the next gig was Ware College; rumour had it, that it was sold out, our first sell-out. Which was a massive ego hit for all of us, that is, until we found out that the tickets sold were a pound each, and remembered that the student bar was subsidised. None of us cared though, so what, we thought. It doesn't matter how we fill the place up. It's that we fill the place up, and with the low entrance fee combined with a cheap bar, people will be totally off their nuts before we go up on stage. Alcohol and more alcohol; It was the perfect warm-up act for us.

On the Saturday afternoon of the gig. Whiff had arranged to meet a girl, he had chatted up at a party in Ware, so with Whiff being the way he was about his women, and Andy having a fight at his boxing club on the Friday night before the gig, we decided to have our last practice on the Friday night, the week before. It wasn't ideal, leaving it a week. We liked the last practice, everyone was buzzing, looking forward to it, thinking what's going to happen this time, and maybe they needed one more practice just to make sure, but no one was that bothered, we were confident, we knew our set inside out by now. A Friday night practice at the pavilion wasn't a problem, either, as the powers that be at Thundridge Football Club, or T.H.C., as Whiff and me called them, had long since given up trying to monitor what we were up to; they were just happy we weren't out in their village hassling people, smashing things up, or causing trouble.

Dave opened the door to the pavilion on Friday night with Bob's key, and we trooped in under the weight of our gear. It seemed colder inside here than outside. I exhaled an icy blast.

"Oh what, it's fucking freezing in here Dave, is there no heaters?"

Dave snorted, placing his bass drum carefully on the floor; the Virus V1 skull grinning at me from its side.

"I can ask Bob if you want? But I know what his answer will be."

"Bollocks?" I ventured.

"I can't perform in conditions like these … I'm an artiste," said Andy, blowing on his hands.

Whiff slouched in with the rest of Dave's drum kit in his arms.

"Cor its fucking freezing in here," he said, exhaling an icy plume.

I smiled, "Yeah Bob's going to sort us out with some heaters, isn't he Dave?"

"Yeah, we've got carpets and curtains coming too," came Dave's voice from behind the grinning skull.

Whiff laughed. "Oh, that would be simply darling," he Celia Johnson-ed, pulling out his baccy pouch.

"Who's this girl you're meeting Saturday then Whiff, do we know her?" I quizzed him, knowing there could be a few laughs to be had.

"No, don't think so, I met her up at a party in Fanham's Hall Road, she was up there with a group of her mates."

"Ooh Fanham's Hall," Andy echoed in a posh accent, "It's well posh up there."

"Is it Lady Fanham?" I grinned.

"Lady Fanny?" Andy asked.

Whiff laughed, shook his head, smiled indulgently, "Nah, her name's Steph."

I looked to Dave, slapped my hand onto my forehead, "Oh no, not another one."

Dave pulled his jaw down, grimacing playfully.

Whiff sparked up a roll-up, cackled, "You know what the first thing I said to her was?"

I saw my chance and took it, shot back, "That you liked her because she was like a maaan?"

"No, no, no… it's worse than that," Whiff took a huge toke of his roll-up, took it all down, taking his time, then blew out an icy cloud of smoke. "I said… I said, nice legs, shame about your face," and we all fell about laughing.

Dave spun a drum stick above his head and repeated incredulously, "Nice legs, shame about the face… Oh dear, oh dear, oh dear, is that a new pick-up line now?"

"I can't wait to try that one out, 'I like your legs, but you've got a face like a horse's arsehole," I said, through tears of laughter.

Dave chuckled and playfully hit his head with the drumstick, "Bloody hell, I don't know, most blokes would say something like you look nice or maybe do you want a drink? But nice legs shame about the face... Bloody hell, come on mate, you have to have a modicum of decorum here, don't you Whiff?"

Andy grabbed his mic, sang, The Monks' song, "Nice legs, shame about the face, nice legs, shame about the face, nice legs, shame about the face, nice legs, shame about the... Boat race," and soon we all joined in, creasing up laughing at our mate, who sat there in clouds of smoke watching us, puffing away contentedly, nodding along.

"No, hold on, hold on," said Dave at the end of our singsong. "So, let's get this straight..." he said, pointing his drumstick accusingly at Whiff. "You said, 'nice legs, shame about the face' and, she heard you... And she agreed to meet you?"

Whiff casually took a puff on his roll-up, "Yep."

"Is she a bit slow or something?" Dave asked.

"A bit deaf, dumb and fucking blind, I reckon," I said, grabbing Whiff's baccy pouch, fishing out a ready-made.

Dave creased up, "That's a little bit harsh, isn't it Skin?"

I looked over to Andy.

"Harsh realities of life, my friend…" We replied in unison.

Whiff watched the ongoing show with a huge smile etched onto his face.

"Look at him, he doesn't give a shit," Dave laughed.

"Yeah, and we all know why, don't we? … The dirty bastard," I said, lewdly.

"Andy doesn't," said a smiling Whiff.

Andy shrugged his shoulders. "Whiffy, barmy army, Whiffy, barmy army, Whiffy, barmy army," he sang, at the top of his voice, punching his fist up into the air raising the roof, and not long afterwards, Dave and me joined in too.

Whiff said, "Yeah, yeah, OK, ha, ha," enjoying every minute of our impromptu homage to him.

"Come on, we better get on," I said, noticing the time.

Virus V1 launched into the set, it was so good to be back playing with my mates, playing with the band again. It's a clique, but it really was like a breath of fresh air. In came Andy, Whiff, Dave; my mates with the music, and out went all the bullshit, the Cannon's, the Stampy's, Mr. fucking Laughter, and that bitter wanker on the bus, 'cheers, you shitter' he said, well, all of them could fuck off now: I had music. Inside me, it flowed and as it flowed it repaired, healed, forcing out all the stress, making me feel good again, not just about my life, but the world in general, too- I wasn't lost in music, I was found in it. I glanced up, looking around at everyone lashing into their instruments. Dave, arms a blur, beaming into the distance, Whiff smiling through his cloud, Andy putting the world to rights. It was the same all round, everyone felt it, it was medicine, an insane sanity, that few outside the music world would ever know.

A whole hour went by, and then, with our music therapy completed, we packed up our gear in the corner of the pavilion, ready for Dave to pick it up the next morning in his van. Dave locked up the pavilion, pocketed the keys, and we strolled up the long sweeping pockmarked hill into the oncoming twilight, towards the allotments, where the hardiest of the gardeners silently tended their vegetables in the oncoming frost.

Andy sang, "Nice legs, shame about the face, nice legs shame about the... Boat race."

"I have just got to work that out on guitar, I could do a version on the next Test Tape," I said, looking at Andy, who smiled back, carrying on serenading us.

"Nice legs, shame about the face, nice legs shame about the... BOAT RACE!"

"You could do a Horror Tapes version," said Whiff, unplugging his dwindling roll-up.

Andy stopped, laughed loudly, "Yeah, do that, that would be good."

"What's this Horror Tapes Skin?" Asked Dave, sounding slightly hurt.

"Oh, it's nothing really Dave, it's just some new tracks I did, nothing special, they sound like slow Virus V1 tracks put through a fuzz box, I'll sort you out a copy if you want?"

Dave nodded, happy again, he wasn't like some other drummers I had heard about, he didn't want to just give the drums a good pounding, he wanted to be involved in the songwriting, know what the new material was, see where the band was going- I should have remembered that.

Whiff stroked his chin, "No, Dave it's a bit more different than that, the lyrics are different, not political, and some of the riffs are a bit metal, I like the one about the boy necrophiliac."

"The boy necrophiliac!!! Bloody hell Skin, that won't fit in with the rest of our set, will it?"

"Nah, it's only a bit of a laugh Dave, I wouldn't want to play any of that stuff live."

Andy chuckled, "I reckon we should play nice legs shame about the face, live; we could do it as encore."

"Oh yeah right Andy, that would fit into our set perfectly, wouldn't it?" Said Dave, sardonically.

"Nah, we could do a religious version of it, call it something like 'Nice Christ Legs, Shame About the Boat Race Fuckers?" I suggested, grinning at Andy, I chanted...

"Symbol of religion,
A man in pain

Jesus died with nice legs,
Well, what a shame about the boat race…" creasing up manically.

I stopped at the top of the hill, looked back into
the enveloping twilight.

"You know what, that's hilarious, could be a classic Test Tape filler,
I've got to do a version of that, I'm going back for my guitar… I
don't know why I left it down there in the first place, I'll go mental at
home without it, I need it."

Instantly it went quiet, the three of them watching me intently, not
moving, I thought you lazy bastards, "OK, OK, it's fine, I'll go back
on my own then, you got the key, Dave?"

Dave pulled a smile, "Are you sure?"

"Yeah, it's fine mate, you're seeing Steph, aren't you?" I asked.

"Oh, don't worry about her, she can wait," Dave said dismissively.

Whiff shot me an amused look.

"No, you get on mate, you might get nice Steph tonight," I said,
trying to ignore his look.

Dave smiled wanly, nodded and gave me the key.

On, back down the hill I walked, even at halfway down, I could still
hear Andy singing 'Nice legs shame about the face', as it echoed
around the valley. I smiled to myself, shook my head and plodded
on.

In the late evening light, shadows stretched long and wide along the pavilion's whitewashed sides, trees swept restless in the last breaths of the day, moving them slowly like shadow puppets. It was completely silent, apart from the soft hum of traffic on the A10 in the distance. I pushed the key into the keyhole, twisting it, popping the mortis, pushed the door open and went inside, it was even quieter inside away from the gentle sway of the trees; it was eerie without us all being in there, talking, laughing, making a big racket, shaking the foundations of the pavilion, the silence was deafening.

A chill slowly crept down my spine, something moved in the shadows of our gear, a tap on the window, I span thinking of Stampy, Moley and the violence that was surely coming my way any day soon, only to see a limp branch bowing in the light breeze, gently brushing the frosty pane. I told myself to shut up, get a grip, concentrate my mind, and quickly grabbed my guitar, legged it to the door, locked it, pocketed the key, and began the walk up the hill again.

On the track at the top of the hill next to the allotments, a silhouette appeared. It was moving in my direction. I hesitated, thinking who the fuck is that? Another shiver left my neck and began the long trek down my spine, then oh, thank fuck for that, it's Hayley. I could recognize her from a mile away as she had a funny way of walking, she would sort of glide like a hovercraft.

I waved my guitar at her, she waved back, and we met up at the top of the hill near the gate.

"Oh hi, Skinner," she said. "I'm not sure if I should talk to you."

181

I smiled, "I shouldn't; I'm a known felon."

Hayley stepped back, looked me up and down like she was measuring me up, "I think prison stripes would suit you, you know."

I creased up laughing, "You reckon? Cheers and maybe for accessories, I could have a little mirrored ball on my chain."

Hayley laughed wholeheartedly. "So what happened? Tell me all about the booze blag, Skinner," she asked, looking at me evenly.

"You sure? It's a long story."

"Yeah, go on, David told some of it, I'd like to know the story from the other Kray brother," she said, a smile teasing her red lips.

OK, I thought I've told this a few times now, I love telling this story, it's second nature now. I'm going to make it really funny; no bullshit, just like it was, funny. I told her of Danny's wild claim about the whisky stash, about Ronnie's 'I'm in' comment, his smoke ring and Dave's reaction, the five of us being so pissed it was a wonder we even found Dawkins' place, the botched burglary and of course when Cannon and Ball the edgy northern teatime entertainers had come to call at my house. I told her about Cannon the wanker making himself comfortable on my couch and then, finally, Peter Ball's awkward rocking chair landing, when he almost ended up on his arse. Hayley was in hysterics by now, leaning forward, leaning into me, close, really close. I was suddenly aware of how close she actually was, and how beautiful she was. I was enchanted by her, by the way the last glimmer of the light of the day teased her Kim Wilde blonde hair, and how her big green eyes steadily held mine. I felt a tingle, like I had inadvertently brushed my leg onto an electric fence. I shuddered in the green beams, breathed her in.

"You know what, you're kind of cute you know, Skinner," she said, moving forward, kissing me on the cheek, then before I knew anything else, she began to kiss me passionately on the lips.

I thought, I must be dreaming here. Aren't I? This is Hayley. My hands tentatively rubbed at her thighs, then moved hungrily around to her firm peach like arse. No, I'm not dreaming this at all, this is real, this is brilliant. It far outshines some of the dreams I've had about her in the night, the ones I woke up to in the morning, feeling ashamed about.

I pulled away, catching my breath, "Whoa, I'm kissing Hayley!"

She laughed, "And I'm kissing Skinner."

"Urgh!" I said, grinning.

Hayley pulled me back into her, kissing me vigorously on the lips, sending more mini-shocks of electricity around my body. I was blown away, lost in her, working on autopilot, my hands sought out her small, firm breasts, squeezing them, she responded by kissing me even harder.

I produced the keys to the pavilion from my pocket with a flourish, waving them in front of her, "Check it out, I've got the keys to the pavilion, let's go down there."

"OK, come on," she said, her green beams full of mischief.

Hayley kissed me again, took my arm, leading me past the gate onto the gravel track, suddenly, she stopped, "No, you'll tell David."

"Oh what, no I won't," I assured.

"Yes, you will Skinner."

"I won't, it's got nothing to do with him, it's just between me and you," I shook my head vigorously.

Hayley shook her head sadly, looked me right in the eye, green beams blazing, boring into me, analyzing me, gathering information, "I know what David and you are like Skinner; you tell each other everything, I know you will."

"I won't Hayley, why would I?" I said, to her slender back.

Hayley stopped, looked over her shoulder, sighed, then whirled away from me up the hill. One step, two steps, three steps, four steps, five steps, ten steps, fifteen steps; I was distraught, downcast, confused, and more than anything else, frustrated. I thought how cruel life can be, to be so close, and then what was this? She slowed, stopped, stood still for a moment, thinking, more thinking, not moving any further away from me, still thinking, and then. Oh my god she turned around, marched back, grabbed hold of my hand, shone those green beams into mine.

"If you tell him, I'll kill you."

I was sure I wouldn't, "I... I... Won't... I won't, Hayley, there's no way I will." I was dumbfounded.

Hayley nodded, smiled, planted a sweet kiss on my cheek, took my hand, and we set off back down the hill, towards the pavilion, and for me, the only dreamt-about, unobtainable, unpromised land. It was almost pitch black now, twilight had retreated, and darkness had rushed into fill the gap, the only visible light for us now, was the orange arterial glow from the A10 in the distance. Hayley linked her arm in mine, pulling me closer to her and in the blackness, I was aware of how silk like, her skin was as it brushed mine.

"You really are lovely, you know that," I said, breaking our silence.

She snorted, "Oh no, I'm not Skinner."

I couldn't resist it, I pantomimed, "Oh yes you are Hayley."

She cracked up laughing; she was putty in my hands now.

Clare Buttercroft and now Hayley Willaims, I thought fucking hell, I'm turning into the stud here.

Once we had made it down the hill, we moved off the stony track, setting off across the soft grass of the cricket pitch, and there in front of me lay the now-promised land, shining white at the edge of the pitch. It was beautiful, it was close, no more than twenty paces away now.

"I'm not lovely, Skinner," Hayley said, stopping.

"Oh yes you…"

I peered questioningly into her face, "What's the matter Hayley?"

Hayley looked down. "No, no, no," she said to herself, having finally worked out what the consequences of her actions might be.

Hayley nodded to herself, she was back in control now, she knew what she had to do, she looked up apologetically into my confused face.

"What? What is it?" I asked, fearing the worst.

"I'm sorry, Skinner," she said, planting her soft lips onto mine for one last time as an apology, and then, with nothing more to say, or do, she turned away from me and the promised land.

Onto the cold grass under my feet my dreams, splintered, then shattered. I stood motionless, mouth agape, watching as she slowly glided back up the hill, away, into the darkness, then she disappeared completely, along with my raging hard on. I felt confused, downcast, frustrated, angry, irritated, unbelieving, disappointed, lost and then confused all over again; I wasn't confused about one thing though, I knew she wasn't coming back this time.

In bed that night, I went over it again, trying to work it out, it just didn't make any sense to me, there was no way I would have told Dave. I had two very good reasons to keep it quiet.

One, if I kept schtum, I might be able to visit the unpromised land again, maybe and again and again, now that would have been something; Imagine that! I felt a stirring from under the covers, I thought, and you can fuck off, if it wasn't for you, I wouldn't be feeling like this now.

Two, if I did tell anyone, Aaron the Ted would more than likely get to hear about it, which would mean the cock and bollocks that had got me into all of this in the first place would get liquidized, pulverized, flattened under one of his size twelve brothel creepers. I just couldn't work it out in my mind. Why did she change her mind once she had made her mind up for the second time? Why? Maybe it was my fault, there was that moment when we walked in silence, maybe if I had kept nattering. She might not have had time to think it over again, oh fucking hell, was that it? I fumbled, choked on the last lap? I would never know now.

I rolled over ignoring the little head's sticky presence, trying to forget about it, gave some thought to our up-and-coming gig at Ware College… Maybe if I would have just gone for it there and then up the top of the hill by the gate. What? Nah, what about the people at the allotments. Fuck off, gone for it up the top by the gate? You weren't in control there, you were……

In the twilight zone, I walked up to the pavilion door, the security lights flicked on, making me jump, making me aware she was next to me, smiling, her green eyes pulling me in like tractor beams.
I produced the key from my front pocket, opened it, and she glided into the scattered darkness. I followed her into the pavilion's main hall, trying to ignore the guilt being thrown out by Dave's drum kit that lay silent in the corner. I watched her silhouette, slender shoulders, Kim Wilde spiked hair strobe on and off in the stuttering glare thrown by the lights outside. A cherry red fingernail beckoned me into the changing room; I was powerless, floated towards her, watching as she began to undress. I felt the electricity searing through my longing body, rising up, filling it with light, imploding, imploring and moved quickly to her: I wasn't going to miss my opportunity this time. I puckered up to kiss her; all of her. She

turned and before me was the wizened face of the old bag
from The Founder's Hall gig.

"I think your Music is dIsgusting, disgustinG, disgusting…
DIIIISSSGUUUSSTING!" She screamed into my stunned face.

"Aaaaaaaaaaaaahhhhhhhhhhhh!" I screamed back.

DIIIIISGGGGUUUUSTING, DIIIIIISGGGGUUUUSTING,
DIIIIIISGGGGUUUUSTING!

I recoiled, bolted, run out of the changIng room, tripping
over Dave's drum kit in the main hall, cymbals crashing
everYwhere. In amongst the detritus, the Virus V1 logo
on the bass drum openED its jaw, grins, laughs and
shouts. 'Why are you trying to fuck My older sister
Skin?' 'I wasn't, honestly, it was her!' 'Oh fuck off mate,
don't give me that, you knew what was going on, how do
you think I'd feel about it?' It tells me. 'Fuck off!' I kick
it hard, ineffectually. It laughs Some more, 'fine fucking
mate, you are matey'. I leg it from the skUll's cackling
madness, findIng myself at the beginning of a lOng
corridor, a glimmering exit sign at its end. It's the new
promised land, I think, a land of forgiveness, clemency, a
new beginning, sanctuary; I need to Get to it now, I run
tOwards the light, but the exit disaPpears into the
distAnce, getting further and further away. I run
faster, faster, faster, my legs blurrIng, passing the two

littLe kids from Flounders Hall who look up and chant in unison, 'Christ fuckers! Christ fuckers! Christ fuckers!' At mY pathetic fleeing fRame. I see the door, my way out, it is right in front of me... I'm there. I pull down on the handle: it's locked... It's locked, it's fucking locked...... Behind me, the corridor shuDders, the sound of pounding boots, The Wolf Pack on the march, military assault, operation sea lion. Blood-red boots running over scorched crimson soil, cattle trucks rolling, six million die in vain. I shiver, tearing at the handle, feel cold bReath on the back of my neck, see the pHlegm hit the door, laugHter, more laughter... I pull doWn even harder on the paralYsed handle, panic rising. Stampy's boot smashes down on my hand, obliterating it.

"AAhhhhhhhhhh no, no fucking hell, no get off iiiiiiiiimmmmmmmmmmmm!"

I sat bolt upright in bed, breathing hard, my bedroom, my sanctuary spreading its calming hands around me, heard my mum's voice calling my name "Mike, Mike," excitedly from downstairs, calming me more, I rubbed my head, trying to erase the images from my aching head.

I've got to start taking the seeds out that sensi before I smoke it, I thought.

"What? What now?" I replied, groggily.

"Mike, you've got an official-looking letter, it's here on the table," she informed me.

"Hey Mike, come on, let's see what it says," said the old man, his voice positively singing.

Oh no, here we go, I thought, what if that tosser, Mr. Laughter, actually gave me the job. Nah no chance, surely not, I fucking hope not. I'll go mad working there, serving the machines; I can't even escape in my dreams anymore. It was time for reality, so chucking my feet out of my damp twisted blankets, I yawned and padded off downstairs to see what all the fuss was about.

On the table in the kitchen, propped up against a teacup sat a brown envelope with Ashwell Printers L.T.D; the h in Ashwell smudged over, making it look like Asswell Printers. I smiled to myself, opened it, knowing full well what was inside and read aloud:

"Dear Mr. Baker,

Thank you for coming in to interview for this position, as you may know, we interviewed a number of candidates for the position of apprentice print operative. I regret to inform you that after careful consideration, wa... I think that should say we, so yeah, we, cannot offer you this job at this point in time, however in future..."

"I knew it, I bloody knew it," said the old man, angrily snatching the letter from my grateful hands. He gave it a quick scan. "I bet he didn't even bloody try," he said, raising his voice, pointing at mum accusingly.

Mum surveyed my face.

"I don't know what happened, maybe they wanted someone with experience?" I lied, trowelling on the bullshit.

"Oh yes, here he is, the bullshitter, bullshitting the bullshitter," said the old man, chucking the letter on the floor. "Bloody waste of space."

I went to protest, but he wasn't having any of it, he dossed me out menacingly, pointed aggressively, "I'm telling you this now, this is your last warning, you get a job, or you're going to be a lot of trouble, the world will run you into the ground… The way you're going, you're going to end up in London sleeping under Hungerford Bridge with all the other tramps, and guess what boyo? That won't be my problem… That will be your problem."

Oh, here he goes again, I thought, what is it with bloody Hungerford Bridge? I suppressed a laugh, thinking of the Lilo I would need to stop me from sinking into the deep, dark, depths of The River Thames, when he stopped by the door on his march-out, scrutinizing me like he was reading my mind, then he scowled some more, span, and slammed the door behind him.

I sat down with Mum, "Mike, you've got to get a job, it's gone on for too long now."

"I am working mum, I'm gardening, I'm paying my keep here, more than paying my keep here… And I'm working with the band too, we're going to do a demo tape, send it to record labels, punk labels, we've got some more gigs coming up, we could get signed any time soon."

"Yes, yes, I understand that, but that could take an age, Mike."

"Yeah, it could do, I suppose, it might not though, you never know."

Mum gave me an indulgent look.

I sighed, shook my head, looked away, knowing she was right, "I heard the Manpower Services are starting another archaeological dig in spring, we'll be signing a one-year contract this time, so they'll have to see it through."

Mum shook her head sadly, "I don't think so, Mike. It's months off, and it might not happen at all, you know how tight things are now?" She moved uncomfortably in her seat, "You've got to find something now, Dad's had enough, what do you want to do?" Quickly quantifying it, "Outside of music, that is."

"I don't know," I said, and I didn't, I really didn't know what I wanted to do,

"I'm sorry, Mum, I wish I knew, I just need a bit more time, the band's going well."

"Dad's retired, he just wants to make the most of the time he has left, there is no more time."

Mum and me sat in silence for a while, letting the dust settle, "I've an idea, why don't you do your driving test, then that'll give you more options, it might help you out with the band too?"

"Yeah, yeah that's a good idea, Mum, I was talking about it
to Dad the other day."

Mum brightened, "OK, good, good, that's settled then. It won't be
cheap though, I had some lessons last year, and it costs ten
pounds per lesson, it's very steep." She cautioned, her face clouding
over again,

"I can pay half though?"

"Yeah? Are you sure?"

She smiled broadly, "Yes, of course."

I could do five pounds a week, I thought, I don't know what I would
do without you, mum, "Cheers mum, that would be brilliant."

Mum laughed excitedly, "OK let's do that, it's a small price to pay, to
keep the peace," she said wisely, and both feeling a lot better
now, we shared a peaceful breakfast together.

Chapter 10

Where Egos Shouldn't Dare

I thought it would be a good idea to keep out of the old man's way
for a while, so he could cool off a bit. I couldn't be bothered with
another one of his silly predictions of my future residency
underneath Hungerford bridge. In fact, I thought, if I heard that load
of old bollocks just one more time. I was more than likely to tell the
stupid old git to piss off for once and for all, which would have
made everyone's life in the Baker household a lot worse. It was time
for a tactical retreat, so I retreated up to my bedroom, up
into the sanctuary, away from the resident doom-laden
Nostradamus, for the afternoon, to finish another new track that I
had been working on called 'Church War'. 'Church War' was a
rousing, upbeat number with an intro, instrumental part and an end
sequence which I had lifted from a classical piece called 'In the Hall
of the Mountain' by Edvard Grieg that I had heard on the TV. I was
really pleased with it, as not only did I think it was some of the best
music I had ever written, lyrically, I thought it was strong too.

'Christ can suffer in his own crude way,
I don't give a fuck about him anyway,
He can hang on his cross for the rest of time,
He may get someone's soul, but he won't get mine.'

'They make the wars, you pay the cost,
Hear the same thing in a church or mosque,
The same old shit, the same old lies,
Leaving the dead meat for the flies,
They say he died to save us all,

194

Believe in us or you will fall.'

'Church war, Church war, Church war, Church war,
 Church war, Church war, Church war, Church war.'

'Look at the wars your church creates,
it's obvious to see that Jesus hates,
he hates, he hates, he hates… You.'

I wrote a lot of anti-religious tracks. It was easy for me, as I hated all
organised religions with a passion, the way they twisted the truth,
used lies and superstition to control people who were either
uneducated or too scared to question the prevarication of that which
was laid out before them. In essence, to me, all religions were a kind
of spiritual police force, set up by the rich and powerful to
protect their interests; an all-seeing, guilt provoking, yoke around
people's necks that kept them pliable, subservient and ultimately
downtrodden, while the select few, the self-chosen ones, could carry
on in any debauched and foul way that they saw fit.

Once I had taken 'Church War' as far as I could on my own,
without the band's input, I leaned my guitar back against the wall,
keys out, and noticed that while I had been diligently working, the
afternoon had gone, disappeared, and darkness had crept in outside.
I stood up feeling hungry, thinking, hoping, that most of 'storm, old
man' would have blown itself out by now, so breaking cover, I went
downstairs to see if I could rustle up a bit of grub.

On the way downstairs, I heard the TV blaring out from the lounge,
so forgetting my empty stomach for a moment, I wandered into the
racket trying to look casual, and after moving the sleeping George
off my seat, who stretched expansively as I airlifted him onto the

settee, I sat down and wished I hadn't; I should have gone straight
to the kitchen. It was that time again. It was six o'clock. It was time
for the news, and the old man was in full flow arguing
with the newsreader as usual, and unsurprisingly, as
usual, the newsreader was totally oblivious to his sharp, incisive
criticisms, and unperturbed, he just carried on reading the news like
he couldn't hear a blind word the old man was saying.

Mum nodded me a silent hello, raised her eyebrows. I returned it,
gave her a withering look, and she dived back into her book, to avoid
the flow of righteous indignation.

"Hey Pudge," he said, using his pet name for her, "Look at this big
pile of dog turd on television."

Mum lifted her head, " Errrgh, Tony Benn!!! Hell's teeth!!! I don't
know why you bother to watch it, politicians, they are all a bunch of
charlatans, yuk, I'd rather watch the test card."

"Oh, hi Mike, just in time, watch this: I love the zapper," he said,
picking up the TV remote, and with one touch of the red button, he
commanded, "Sod off," and Tony Benn's face shrunk, and vanished
into the black void, leaving the lounge quiet, and the old man's blood
pressure lower.

I thought bloody hell, that's a surprise, he seems to be in a good
mood this evening. Oh shit, this could only mean one thing, trouble;
what's his next move going to be? If he wants me to reapply to
Asswell printers again, I'm going to tell him to piss off, go down
Dave's.

"Aaaah that's a lot better. It's all bad news these days, every day. Bad news. The way the bloody unions are going on, we won't have a car industry left, strike after strike after strike. Red Robbo, Derek Robinson, communist bastard. Typical socialist; always looking for a handout. Socialism, it's just greed and envy. You know, we beat the Germans and the Japanese in the war, and believe you me, I've got the scars to prove it… And these bastards in the unions are letting them beat us economically. Destroying our heavy industries, so the Japs can just walk in and sell their cars to us. Bloody Japanese. I was on a ship that brought the men who worked on the Burma railway home, well, what was left of them. It was horrific, like they'd been in Bergen-Belsen, skin and bone they were, ten stone men turned into skeletons, and now these slope headed bastards are all smiles selling their cars to the mugs. British Leyland are absolute rubbish, but I would rather drive rubbish, rather than bloody Japanese cars; the murdering bastards."

Jesus Christ, I can't listen to this, I thought, jumping up, giving the now-awake, purring George a pat on the head, left for the kitchen, hoping, there's one of those chow mein pot noodles left.

"Oh, hold on, Mike, mum said you were interested in taking driving lessons, I think driving lessons is a good idea," he said, pulling himself back from the brink of a myocardial infarction.

I nodded, "Yeah, I think it could help get me a job" I said thinking, oh not so bad. It would be a great help with the band, take some of the pressure off Dave, it would be about time, too.

"It might help with the band too?" He offered, playing me at my own game. "Once you've passed your test, you can go into Hertford and go to the discos they have over there," he added, overdoing it now.

I smirked to myself and thought 'discos' that's one good reason not to pass my driving test.

"Yeah... It'll be good to get about," I nodded, letting it go.

"You could go anywhere; it would give you some more of that freedom you're always going on about, Mike," said the old man, placing the magic zapper at his feet, keeping it close.

I nodded genially, thinking, yeah, absolutely, this could be brilliant. I could take Andy, Whiff and Dave up London to gigs if the bands weren't coming to Bowes, and maybe we could go down to the coast for the day too, have a few beers, check the beach out, that would be a right laugh.

"I'll tell you something for nothing, though," he said, revving up again, disturbing my ruminations. "And you should listen to this, Mike, those driving instructors are rip-off artists, they charge thirty pounds for an hour, thirty pounds just to teach people to bloody drive, thirty pounds a bloody hour, they make over two-hundred-and-fifty pounds a day for bloody driving a bloody car, can you imagine that?"

I sighed and protested, "Oh what? No, they're not, they're not thirty pounds, they're ten pounds, Dad."

"I don't know how they get away with it- thirty pounds an hour! Thirty! Just think of it: thirty pounds... For one hour, it's daylight robbery it is... They are taking people for a ride," he blathered on, ignoring me.

Inwardly, I groaned, thinking, well, yeah, people are getting in a car with them, of course they are taking them for a ride; quite literally. I shot a look at mum, who was watching him, probably worrying about his blood pressure again, and the twinkle in her eyes told me that she had heard it too. He hadn't though, and even if he had, I doubted it would've stopped him. It was full steam ahead now, foot on the accelerator, he was in full flow and there was no stopping him. On and on he went, it was a turkey shoot, his intended targets lined themselves up accordingly and accordingly, he shot them down bang, bang, bang.

One after another, the bastards at the DVLA, the Department of Transport and those parasites at the Home Office all came a cropper, it was an incredible assault, I sat wondering, when it was going to end; if it was going to end, and I actually began to think, who is he talking too? It was only George the cat, mum, and me in the room. George the miracle cat had gone back to sleep, mum was deep into her book, and I had stopped listening ages ago, thinking about another verse for 'Church War'. Then finally the storm blew over, and he got back to something relevant.

"I'll tell you what… I can take you out, I'm a good driver, and I'll teach you how to drive properly too, not like those parasitic driving instructors, with their thirty pounds an hour, come on, I'll show you the controls, come on."

"Er yeah OK, if you're sure," I asked, hauling myself up. He was already on his way, though.

I knew my old man was a good driver; like most kids, I had watched him from the back seat taking it all in, and as I got older, I began to appreciate his skill in reading the road ahead, the speed and dexterity of his gear changes and his all-round 'road craft' as he called it.

Once out on the road, he was dynamic, a decent driver, brilliant in fact. I had seen it with my own eyes on many occasions, he could burn up cars with twice the engine size of our Mini 850, leaving them for dust. As for him being able to pass his vast knowledge onto me, I wasn't so sure. He'd taken Mum out a few times over the years, which more often than not, ended up in blazing rows, doors being slammed and uncomfortable silences throughout tea.

In the end, Mum's driving aspirations came to an abrupt halt after one particularly bad lesson, when she came back into the house clearly shaken and conceded to me that, 'she was useless', 'not worth teaching', and 'it was far too late for her as she was too old to learn to drive', which didn't sound like her words, so consequently she gave it up. I didn't like some of the things I believed he had said to her. Mum could be nervy when it came to 'things of a practical nature', but ultimately it sounded like he had put her off driving, put her off for good. It didn't bode well for me, but I was still going to go out with him though, my reasoning being, that there was nothing to lose, and even if I only had a few lessons with him. In the long run, it could save Mum and me a few quid, so dutifully I followed him out into the garage.

Inside our connected garage, he pulled an old blanket off our mustard coloured Mini 850, like a conjurer doing a magical trick. He then carefully folded it, placing it safely onto his workbench, opened the passenger door, hopped inside, and beckoned me to join him. I nodded enthusiastically, slid into the driver's side for the first time since sitting in Dave's 1600e, and my first driving lesson ever began in earnest. It was as I had expected, the information came thick and fast, fast and thick, from the internal workings of the combustion engine to servicing it, driving it, even washing it. He told me everything, his reckoning being that if he taught me everything now, then it would save me time and money later. I found it hard keeping up with the weight of information being tossed in my general direction, there was quite literally tons of it. I wanted to zone out, but I thought, no, he's good, he knows what he's talking about and if I trust him, I could be out on the road by summer, so I concentrated, taking in as much as I could.

Once he had pointed out all the controls; told me what they did, how they did it, why they did it, when they did it, and why they were all an intrinsic part of the running and the driving of a motor car on the roads of Great Britain, we got down to 'the practical side of it'. He had me 'depressing the clutch', 'putting it into gear' 'giving it a bit of gas', then raising my foot to the 'biting point' and 'then slowly letting the clutch out'. I soon forgot about the 'why', 'when's' and 'how's' and concentrated on what was in front me, and after a couple of smooth gear changes, I felt confident I was ready to take on the open road.

"I'm ready, I want to give it a proper go Dad, can we go out now?"

He thought about it for a moment, then shook his head, "No, it's getting dark now, it's a totally different ball game when it gets dark, it's not for the inexperienced, we better wait until tomorrow."

"OK Dad, yeah that's fine… I'm really looking forward to it."

I was too. I didn't know what I had been worried about.

*

On a Monday night, The Anchor was usually dead, so Dave
suggested we take the 1600e out for a spin and see who was about in
Ware, and with driving and driving lessons already on my mind, I
was even more up for it than I usually was. I sunk back into the E's
deep, comfortable seats and watched the fields scroll by with GBH's
'Sick Boy' blasting out from the Blaupunkt speakers on the back
rack. I wound down the window, took a deep breath of the chilly
evening air, thinking, this is brilliant, I need this, and the old man's
right. It could just be the kind of freedom that I have been searching
for, I've just got to learn to drive, it won't be too long.

Dave and me did a couple of pacey, smooth circuits of Ware. It was
just as we expected it to be, we saw nothing and no one of interest, it
was completely dead. Dave turned the E for home, and we charged
back up to the village again, had a scout around there. It was just
the same thing; nothing and no one, nowhere and boredom. So
admitting defeat, we went back to Dave's, where he parked the E
back up underneath the car port at the front of his house, and we
stepped out already feeling exhilarated after the 1600cc engine had
done the business down the A10.

Monday night was a night of being broke, a night of relaxation,
contemplation, and in some cases a night of regret for what they had
got up to over the weekend. Dave and me weren't that bothered. In
fact, it was good having a quiet night out of the pub, chatting
under the car port, as it gave us both a chance to talk through some
of our problems. If one of us broached a subject, no matter what it
was, then the other would listen, try to advise, maybe just listen, as
sometimes a friendly ear was all it took to repair the damage done. In
the years that we had been mates, our chats had certainly helped me
straighten a few things out in my mind, and I hoped it was the same

for Dave, too. If we were both OK and the world was good with us, we would piss about, have a laugh, talk about the band, talk about the future, recently though, our car port conversations were mostly spent talking about Steph, which wasn't my favourite subject.

I pulled out a ready-made roll-up out of my baccy pouch, sparked it up, took a long drag, inhaling and wondered whether he was going to talk about her again tonight.

"I don't know, Skin, it just feels like something's going wrong with me and Steph at the moment, we still see each other a lot, but it's not the same as it was when we first got together, something's wrong, I can feel it," Dave sighed, leaning back on the E.

I exhaled and thought, yep, he is, and it sounds like he needs to talk about her again. So, OK, let's see if I can help him out. I was still friendly with Steph's sister Jill, despite Bentsod the canine exploding milk churn, and my knowledge of Dave's out-of-hours, one-in-hole with her at Chadwell Springs golf course. Jill and me had had a chat only just recently, and she had told me that her mum was feeling down, she'd stopped eating and hadn't spoken to anyone for days.

"I don't know, mate, maybe she's got problems at home; you know what her Mum's like?" I suggested.

Dave nodded, scratched his at chin thoughtfully, "Yeah, could be that, her Stepdad's a bit of a prat too."

I expelled another frosty plume of smoke into the chilly night air, "Oh yeah, how is Jeremy Beadle these days?" I asked, seeing my chance of lightening the conversation.

Dave looked confused, "What? Why Jeremy Beadle?"

"You know, he's got a small hand," waving my full-sized hand up in his face.

"Ohhhh, that's why he wears that stupid fucking glove all the time."

I nodded, "Well he's not Michael Jackson, is he, mate?"

Dave grinned back at me, shaking his head slowly.

I blew out a ghostly smoke ring,

"And what David doesn't know is that Steph's Dad has got a little withered hand," I said, in a poor attempt at Jeremy Beadle's voice on Game for a Laugh, cracking up laughing.

Dave's eyes twinkled back in the darkness, he pulled his car keys from his jacket pocket, dropped them to the floor theatrically and quipped, "A little hand here?"

I sniggered, "Hold up, I'll get Steph's Stepdad," sending us both into hysterics.

Dave picked up his keys, returned them to his pocket, shook his head. "No, it's not the family, it's something else, something's changed, I can't work it out," he said, getting back to it.

On and on it went. Dave and Steph's relationship tales of woe, it was baffling, I puffed my way through two more roll-ups and still we couldn't work out what the problem was, and then he told me that every Thursday night she played badminton with a male colleague from work.

"I wouldn't like that, Dave." I cautioned him.

"I know, I don't like it either... But I'm not her jailer, I can't tell her not to go, can I?"

"I suppose not mate, it doesn't sound right to me though," I said, taking another roll-up out of my fast-dwindling baccy pouch, placing it between my lips.

Dave nodded thoughtfully, "I know, I know, the thing is, she's known him since they were kids, went to junior school together, so she says they're just mates."

I sparked up rollie number four, "It's possible, mate, if they've known each other that long, and they haven't got together, they probably are just mates... I still don't like it though, mate."

Dave pulled a tight smile, shrugged, and put his palms up, "I don't know, I suppose it could be anything, really... Women, eh?"

I shrugged, tapped the ash from my rollie onto the gravel floor of the car port,

"I wouldn't know mate,"

"Oh yeah sorry Skin, listen, we've been talking about Steph and me for ages; what about you? Is there anything happening with you and Clare?"

"Nah, there's nothing going on there, mate, you know what
her Stepdad's like, he's worse than Beadle, the wanker's got her
locked away like Rapunzel, I haven't seen her since you saw us
together that night."

Dave repeated, "Rapunzel," laughed,

"Oh yeah, she plied you with drink all night and took advantage of
you," he said.

I cackled, whined, "I just feel so used,"

Dave snorted.

"I wish she'd, use me again," I said mournfully, gazing at the orange
glow of my rollie.

"I bet, she's well tasty that Clare."

"Yeah, I know, fucking, do I? Oh, well. It wouldn't work anyway,
Dave, we come from two different worlds, can you imagine me
walking into her office, with all those yuppies, I would have probably
ended up pissing in their Perrier water or Fucks Biz; the yuppy
wankers."

A car went racing past us, momentarily taking our attention.

"Oh yeah, I've got some good news for you," Dave said, "I was
talking to Diane a few days ago, and she said Cerys isn't happy with
Mark."

I straightened up, "Oh yeah? What happened? Did he gas her with
his hair lacquer?"

Dave laughed, "What's that you called him? Pepe Le Pue?"

"Yeah, that's it, what did she say then?" I asked, trying to sound casual.

Dave shrugged his shoulders, "I don't know, really, she just said she was a bit bored with him that's all."

I smiled, "I can't say I'm surprised mate, she's had the best, so what does she expect?"

Dave studied me carefully, knowing I was putting on a front.

"I can't see that happening after fucking whisky time, can you?" I sighed, sadly acquiescing.

"No maybe not, she was really pissed off wasn't she... Who else is there?" He asked, brightening.

I flicked another ash build up off my rollie, "Dave, seriously, I can't think of anyone off the top of my head."

He laughed, "Oh Jesus, it's not that bad, is it?"

"Yeah, yeah, it is, Dave," I replied, blowing out another icy fresh plume.

Dave countered, "Oh come on, there must be someone else, who else is there?"

"I don't know mate, to be honest there's not much choice living in a village this size, is there? If you're not into incest, that is."

He sniggered, "Yeah, well, true, OK I tell you what, if you could have any girl in the village who would you go for?"

"Cerys."

Dave laughed, "I knew you were going to say that, even the old bag from The Flounder's Hall gig knew you were going to say that, and she doesn't know either of you."

I laughed nervously, thinking of her twisted face screaming in my dream.

DIIIiiiIIIISSSSSSGgGUUuuUUUSSsSSSTTTTIIIIiNG!

Dave continued, "OK, not including Cerys, someone else?"

I thought about it for a while, then shook my head, "Nope, there's no one."

"What about Jill?"

"Nah mate, she's OK, she's a bit square though,
anyway Bentsod wouldn't allow it," I joked, sparing him the truth that I didn't want to follow in his knob's, knob steps.

"Oh, come on, Skin, there must be someone, what about your neighbour, Lucy Harrington? She's alright, she is, isn't she? She used to get the coach with my little sister Jo?" He said, exasperatedly.

I creased up laughing, "Nah, no chance there Dave... I saw her recently, she said she didn't want to talk to me, called me deviant, told me to sod off."

Dave cracked up, "Bloody hell Skin, why?"

"You remember I told you about Tarnia Gorden's party? She found out that we had been pissing in the drinks."

"Yeah, but you told me you didn't piss in the girls' drinks."

"I didn't, but Whiff did. He was pissing in The Pimms all night long, and he called her Skinhead jacket to her face, he totally fucked it up for me."

Dave slapped the side of the E, creasing up in fits of laughter, "Oh dear, oh dear, what about Lee's old girlfriend Karen, he fucked it up for you there too, didn't he?"

I felt a weird yearning sensation in my stomach, maybe lower.

"Nah, not really, Dave, he did me a favour really, I could have been in a lot of trouble, imagine me having a kid now? Fucking nightmare, mate,"

"Oh yeah, the penis fly trap."

I looked down, feeling ashamed, "I shouldn't have called her that, she's got problems, her mum's a drunk, had a lot of boyfriends, I reckon some of them got to her too."

Dave shook his head slowly, "Ohhhh, Jesus, shit, you reckon?"

"Yeah, I know how she looks, how she comes across, but she's just a little kid mate, she's hanging around with Stampy and The Wolf Pack now, I feel sorry for her."

"Hmmm well, feeling sorry for somebody, that's no basis for a relationship, if I was you, I would forget about her, especially if she's hanging around with Stampy, that blokes' a nasty piece of work."

"Yeah, you're right," I said, still looking down into nothing.

"Who else? Come on, who else? There must be someone you like, Skin, come on, anyone, in the village or outside, Ware, Hertford, High Cross, er Cold Christmas… Er Colliers End?"

"I don't know, mate," I said, huffily kicking at some gravel on the ground.

"Come on, anyone? Anybody, there must be someone? Jesus."

"OK, listen, I'll tell you who I like… Don't laugh, but I like your sister."

"What Hayley!?" He asked, incredulously.

"Yeah, she's really nice, I like her."

Dave snorted, "Nooo…… She wouldn't go for you, Skinner." He replied, vehemently.

"Oh, come on, man… You asked, it's hypothetical, yeah?"

"Yeah, hypothetical, but that's hyper-mental… I think we should rule her out of the equation, don't you, old chum? She wouldn't touch you with a barge pole, mate… You've got no chance," He said dismissively, and Alan-ed, "Hayley! Bloody hell mate, have a heart."

I hesitated for a moment, feeling affronted by his temerity, then thought, fuck it, he won't tell her, he probably won't even believe me anyway. Nah, I'll be fine… Nothing happened really.

"I bumped into her after practice on Friday and we…"

Dave cut in, "Oh, yeah?" his brow furrowing, giving me a sceptical look, "Yeah, she said she'd seen you, so what happened then?"

"Dave, please mate, you can't tell her I told you."

A big smile creased his face, "Tell her what? What's all this about Skin?"

"You can't tell her, I told you alright?"

"I won't, I won't."

I took a deep breath. "We ended up kissing," I said, diving straight in.

Dave laughed uproariously, "Bollocks."

I shrugged my shoulders, "OK, what can I say?"

Dave scanned my face for any hint of a grin, finding none, "OK Skin, go on, then what happened?" He said, indulging me.

I told him what happened right from the moment we met at the top of the hill, and as I told him, his indulgent look fell into disbelief, disbelief plummeted into confusion, and finally that confusion turned into shock. He was absolutely dumbstruck by my disclosure.

Once I had finished and pleaded with him not to say anything to Hayley or anyone else for that matter, we stood in silence for what felt like a very long time. A very long time indeed, and as the seconds ground away between us, turning into minutes. I began to think, that even though Dave and me had always told each other everything right from the time we had been at junior school together, I might have made a mistake here, a big fucking one with bells on it.

A car roared past us, cutting through the awkward silence, the awkward silence that I had created, created for no other reason apart from my stupid ego, I thought, I've got to mend this now, right here, right now. I could be losing my best mate here, losing my best mate over a kiss.

"What do you reckon on the Ware college gig then, Dave?" I asked, awkwardly trying to change the subject and, much to my relief, he stopped looking off into the distance.

"It'll be good to be gigging again, especially after the last one, if it's as half as good that I'll be happy," he said, thoughtfully. "It feels like a long time since the last one," he said introspectively.

"I know, mate, a lot's happened since then," I said, meaning the booze blag.

Dave eyed me carefully, "Huh... Well, yeah, it certainly has," he said, meaning Hayley.

"Oh, fucking hell man, I knew I shouldn't have said anything," I said leaning forward, putting my hand on my forehead trying to smother my stupid brain. "I'm sorry Dave, it just sort of happened, OK? One minute we were talking, pissing about, then... I don't know, it just happened, it was only a kiss, one kiss, it was nothing, it's like you said mate, she wasn't interested in me, please don't say anything to her. I promised her, and if Elvis Aaron finds out, it'll not only be Elvis that's left the building, my bollocks will have gone too; no, thank you very much."

Dave grinned, scrutinising me, "I wasn't talking about that. Well, maybe I was... Anyway, look... Don't worry about it, I'm not her keeper, it's up to her what she does, she might be my older sister, but I've got no say in what she does ... In this world, only Hayley tells Hayley what to do, nobody else gets a look in, not even the old man," he told me, finally putting it to sleep.

I pulled a fresh roll-up from my baccy pouch, lit it up, "OK cool mate, as long as we are cool, that's all that matters."

"Yeah, yeah, of course, Skin, of course, let's talk about the gig... Women, eh?"

"Women, eh," I echoed back.

Dave and me, carried on talking like nothing had happened for a while, then noticing I was out of roll-ups, and with a big day of driving in front of me tomorrow, we called it a night.

I wandered back up through the pitch-black churchyard, up my road, and into my house through the back door, where I almost got knocked over by George the miracle cat, as he took his chance to get out of the cold and back into the warm again. I picked him up, stroked him down, got him purring, then took him into the lounge where mum and the old man were seated in front of the TV, watching Mike Yarwood doing his impressions, laughing their heads off. I deposited the still purring, even more contented, George onto mum's lap; said goodnight, and left them to it, went up to my bedroom to play around with some more new guitar riffs I was working on, and then, finally feeling tired, I went to bed early to get ready for the next day.

Chapter 11

Mini Driver; Major Fuck Up

In the early hours of the next morning the old man blasted me out of bed; I didn't care though, because today, I was going to learn how to drive, or at least learn the basics. I had the quickest of washes, then Mum, the old man, and me shared a rare breakfast together. As we ate, the old man wittered on about the DVLA, how it should have stayed in London rather than been moved to Swansea, and after giving the Taffs a huge chunk of his mind. He started going on about how expensive driving lessons were again. I thought about his 'being taken for a ride' comment again, smiling to myself, shook my head at the unintended pun; how could he have not seen that one?

Mum and me shared an amused glance; mum and me loved a pun, especially one that was said without the person knowing it. She didn't much like ranting though, so sensibly, she ducked down, burying her head in a book that she was reading, sparing herself some of the incoming onslaught. It began to get to me too, so I looked around for George - he wasn't in yet though.

On the table in front of me, a smiling Jimmy Savile grinned up from the cover of The Radio Times, Auntie BBC's journal; unable to cope with the old man's vitriol, with a sharp intake of breath I grabbed it, opened it up, buried my head in it, following mum's lead. I wasn't expecting much, and what I got was pages and pages of not much; and then, when I got to the centre page spread, there he was the man himself. Uncle Jimmy, the ex-miner, new Tory. Who despite all the rumours going around, was still a popular entertainer, who was let within inches of children, inches that my mates and me knew that he would like to fill with his withered old dick.

Karen and me had been talking about him one day, back when she was with Lee, before the party in Kings Hill, and she'd told me that, if she went on Jim'll Fix It and met Jimmy Savile, and he had been good enough to give her a ride in his Rolls-Royce; then it would have been the least she could do, to give him a quick hand shandy in the back. I cracked up thinking she was joking, but I wasn't so sure now, having said that, from what I knew now, Jimmy wouldn't have been interested in her; Karen must have been seventeen at the time. I chucked the rag back onto the table, thinking, fucking hypocrites, tuned back into the old man, as he was saying about how the government bled hard-working people like him to death. Stealing their money, wasting it on rubbish for the masses, and layabouts, then at sixty-five years old they said OK you've done your bit, you can retire now. Only for most of them to die, fall early, without seeing their retirement. I thought, yeah, so stop moaning and start living. You've made it, have your retirement before you fall early too, with your blood pressure higher than The Post Office Tower.

"Oh, there he is," the old man said, pausing his rant on the government, pointing at Savile's grinning face on the kitchen table, "Jimmy bloody Savile, the Yeti, do you know they made him an O.B.E. an O.B.E., do you know what that means? It means: The most excellent Order of the British Empire, him? That Yeti, he's a weirdo, O.B.E. Orrible, Bleeding, Erbert more like."

I cracked up laughing, I couldn't help it, he looked back, smiling, too, I knew now, with my encouragement, there would be no stopping him now. I braced myself, hoping it would be the funny ranting rather than the old blood and guts, shoot 'em up, John Wayne crap.

216

"It's the B.B. bloody C Mike, it's full of communist weirdos, and homosexuals, they were all mates with those Cambridge poofs, Maclean, Guy Burgess, Blunt, and Philby. You know while my friends were dying, drowning going down on their ships to save this country from Hitler, they were spying for uncle Joe Stalin. Hitler and Stalin had a pact, the Nazi Soviet pact, so while Hitler was planning to invade our country, they were helping him too, the bloody poofters, we should have hung them before they could defect......"

On and on he went, it wasn't the funny ranting I had hoped for either, not even I could have squeezed a joke out of this deluge of bitter hatred. I was about to say something to stop the cascade of finger pointing misery, when the doorbell rang, I went to get up, but Mum was a lot quicker, and she was already at the kitchen door, even before I was out of my seat, she gave me a satisfied smile and left me to it. A moment later, she came back, fanning a handful of letters; a Giro for me, which I quickly hid between my legs, and the quarterly electric bill, which she tentatively placed in front of the old man. In a shot, she was gone, she ran out of the room like a terrorist who had planted a bomb on a short fuse. It went off soon afterwards.

"Bloody day-light robbery, those bastards, look at this, look at this," he said, thrusting the bill bomb in between me and my cornflakes. I looked it over, it was just a bunch of figures, I couldn't make head nor tail of it, so I shook my head, carried on crunching the golden flakes.

"I don't believe it; how can it be that expensive... Oh yes, I know, how it can be so expensive it's the bloody unions, isn't it, that shit Scargill and his bloody miners, with their massive pay demands, those bloody miners, they did the same thing during both wars, a bunch of traitors they are, while our soldiers were dying those bastards were on strike, at home hiding behind their women's petty coats, well they can stick their coal-fired power stations up their arse. It's polluting the world anyway; we want nuclear power."

On he went still, I clamped my legs around my Giro, keeping it safe, thinking if he sees this the mood, he's in, it would be like a red rag to a bull, he'll probably implode. He kept on leaning forward, though, making me think he knew it was there.

"OK, I'd better get ready," I said, twisting in my seat, slipping my Giro into my back pocket.

"But, oh no, the hippies don't want nuclear power, do they? The bloody idiots. They think it pollutes the world. Can't they see that the smoke from the coal-fired power stations are far worse, they are the ones polluting the atmosphere, with their constant smoke. Scandinavian forests are dying because of the pollution blowing over the North Sea from our power stations, stupid long-haired bloody hippies" he replied, getting to his latest ism, 'the hippies'.

I've had enough of this I thought, so I jumped up, made my great escape, following in mum's footsteps, left him to it, taking my precious Giro with me, up to the peace in my time of the bathroom. Once I had secured the bathroom door, locking it out, I brushed my teeth, threw a bit of water on my face, trying to wake up, trying to keep cool, trying not to think about putting the razor blade down my arm again. It wouldn't have made any difference, just like the last few times, nothing changed. I just couldn't work out what his problem was this morning, yeah, sure, the world could be cruel, and unjust, but why dwell on it? He was supposed to be teaching me, his son, how to drive today, getting me ready for my oncoming independence, in reality, all he was doing is driving me up the fucking wall. I started thinking about proper driving lessons; ten quid an hour was beginning to sound like a real bargain now; even thirty would be good.

I left the bathroom feeling wide awake and minty fresh. It was incredible, I could still hear his cries of anguish from downstairs. So I retired to my bedroom, the sanctum, opened my Giro, thinking it's going to be a pub night tonight, and not only am I going to have a few, I can buy some for my mates and pay them back too. I heard the old man shout for me, so, assuming electrical bill storm old man had blown over, I ventured downstairs. Only to find it was the eye of the storm, and had to endure even more of the turbulence as we walked into the garage.

"It's subsidised by the government, so the unions don't care, they know they could strike forever, and still have jobs. The unions have promised them jobs for life. Why? Nobody has that, not me, not anybody, even Maggie Thatcher hasn't got a job for life. You see, they think the poor taxpayer is a bottomless pit. You know for every ton of coal mined in this country, the taxpayer, i.e., me, bloody muggin's here, pays one pound in my tax, a pound in all of our taxes to subsidise the bloody miners, and then we have to pay for it all over again when it gets put in the coal bunker too, so we all pay for it twice and why? Because of the sodding unions, scum."

"Oh, for god's sake, Dad, can we just concentrate on driving?" I cut in, finally losing it.

"You wait, if we don't get rid of scum like Scargill, Benn, and Red Robbo, we'll have no heavy industry left… No coal, no car, or steel industry, nothing, we'll have millions on the dole."

I blew out my cheeks loudly, deflated them, he turned peering at me.

"Huh!" He said, ripping the blanket off the car, spreading a million particles of dust into the sunshine blazing in through the open garage door. Now look at that, I thought, now that's something worth talking about, reaching out to open the driver's door.

"No, no, no, wait, wait, we've got to do the pre-drive checks first!" He instructed, his voice rising.

I sighed, "I don't think that's in the test, is it?"

"It might save your life one day,"

"Oh, come on, Dad, can we just do the test stuff? We can do that another time."

"Well, yes, alright then," he said, sounding put out,

"Get in then."

Opening the door, I got in, buckled my seat belt.

"I don't believe in them, if we crash, you'll get fried," he said. So I unbuckled it, and watched the metal clip shoot back over my shoulder.

"Oh no, keep it on, keep it on, you'll need it if you want to pass your test," he said, agitatedly.

I sighed long and loud, buckling up again.

"OK now right, I'm going to teach you the proper way to drive, no baby steps with me, if I teach you the advanced stuff now, that'll save you time later."

"I just need to pass the test, Dad; I can learn how to drive afterwards."

The old man cracked up, nodded, "And you will too, right turn the key in the ignition."

I reached forward.

"You know I've never taken a driving test before?" He interjected.

I stopped in my tracks, "Yeah, I know, you told me before."

"I've got what they call a grandad licence, I got it during the war, everything I know is self-taught."

I exhaled loudly, dropping my now heavy head, "I know, shall we get on with this, Dad?" I said impatiently, hoping that he would just shut up.

"OK, OK, are you ready then? Turn the key in the ignition."

I turned the key, the engine stuttered into life, then died instantly.

"What did you do that for?" He laughed. "You didn't pull the choke out, what's the first thing I told you to do before starting the car? Pull the choke out … Well, on cold days, anyway."

I nodded, gently pulling the choke out, turned the engine over again, and again it burst into life, overrunning a bit.

"I can teach you how to double de-clutch if you want?" He boasted.

I sighed again, put my hand to my forehead, and dragged it down my face like I wanted to erase it from existence, "Come on Dad, let's just stick to this, we can do that later."

I depressed the clutch, put the car straight into first.

"No, no, no, wait, wait, what did I tell you about waiting for the engine to warm up, you let the engine warm up then…?" He opened his arms waiting for the answer.

"You put the choke in?"

"No. No. God, no. If you push the choke all the way in, the car might stall, so you push the choke in a little bit and see how the engines idling OK, OK?" He told me, testily.

"OK, OK" I answered tersely, took the car out of gear, pushed the choke in a bit.

"Now listen to the engine. Sounds OK, doesn't it?"

I thought it sounded like our lawn mower compared to Dave's 1600 E's engine.

"Yeah, it sounds good," I said, smirking.

"Put it in gear, let's go."

I pushed the gear stick forward, I couldn't find it this time, so started whisking it erratically backwards and forwards, left and right.

"Jesus Christ, you're pulling that gear stick around like a virgin with her first hot cock," he said, cracking up laughing, at my pathetic attempts.

"Oh ha, ha, very funny, are you ever going to stop going on all the sodding time?" I said, throwing the gear stick forward aggressively.

"Well, there's no need for that, I was only pulling your leg," he said, his face dropping like a stone.

I looked forward down the road. Into the distance. Jealous of how far it was away from where I was right now, thinking I don't know how much more of this I'm going to be able to take.

"Come on then, let's keep going, depress the clutch and put it into first," he said, trying to keep the impatience out of his voice.

"Right," I said, grabbing the gear stick again.

Into first, it went nice and easily this time, so encouraged, I pressed the accelerator down, 'giving it some gas' found the biting point, eased the clutch out. We jolted forwards, then rocked backwards as I took my foot off the accelerator, then somehow, we were off, out of the garage, down our drive, onto our road. I was driving for the first time. It felt good, so I smiled to myself, took a quick sideways glance at the old man to see if he was enjoying it too. Only to see he was boggled-eyed, hands on the dashboard, white knuckles digging in, looking for purchase.

"Slow, down, slow, down!" He urged, his voice rising.

I went for the brake, but my size ten D.M boot depressed the clutch instead, the car pitched forward haphazardly.

"Bloody hell, don't use the clutch, take your foot off the accelerator, use the break," he urged, the panic rising in his voice.

I stamped down hard on the accelerator overreacting, and the car kangarooed violently, throwing us first, backwards then forwards, then forwards and backwards in our seats.

"Watch it, watch it, you're going to stall it, put the clutch in," he shouted, as the car slowed to a crawl.

I pushed the clutch in, but too late, the Mini's 850cc engine crunched, gave out a horrible grinding metallic wail and stalled, died. Leaving us stranded in the middle of the road.

"What did you do that for?" He asked.

"Yeah, like I did that on purpose!" I shot back.

"A car doesn't understand you know, it doesn't have feelings, everything you do in a car is on purpose!"

No really? I thought, and there was me thinking I could give it a bunch of fucking flowers, and it would take me to the next

Discharge gig. For fucks sake, one more comment like that, and I'm going to tell him to stick his driving lessons up his arsehole.

"Live and learn, live and learn," he said evenly, letting go his limpet like grip on the dashboard.

OK, I thought, pushed my rising angst down. I did exactly what he said, put the car back into first, 'gave it a bit of gas', let the clutch out smoothly, and we were off again. Into second, smoothly up into third gear without any problems, and once again we were coasting along quite nicely. I thought, I'll show him, this is easy. I'm the quintessential road user.

Mrs. Harrington's white, Herbie like, Volkswagen Beetle appeared from out of the sun, around the corner at the top of our road and sedately came towards us.

"Oh, NOW, hold on, watch it, WATCH IT, there's a car coming. There's a car coming."

"I know, I know, it's fine Dad, I see it," I said calmly, easing my foot off the accelerator, putting my other foot over the clutch, getting ready to change down as she got closer.

Mrs. Harrington's Herbie like Beetle ambled up to us, going about as fast as an arthritic snail on downers. It was all very civilised, road use at its most civil. On her front window she had placed a CND sticker, I smiled, and thought the old man won't like that. I was about to lift my hand off the steering wheel to give her a wave, when the old man shoulder barged across me, knocking my arm out of the way.
He grabbed the steering wheel, pulling it down hard, making the car lurch left, and it smashed into the kerb, stalled and died.

"Why did you do that?" I shouted.

"You didn't have control of the bloody car, that's why," he shouted back.

"I was OK."

"No, you bloody were not."

I scowled at him, my face full of resentment, full of hate, full of regret that I was stupid even to try this. He returned my glare, and I thought what a complete, and utter, waste of my time this has been. I should have stayed in fucking bed, then just like the last straw dropping onto an overworked camel's back, as the Beetle trundled passed, he looked at Mrs. Harrington, laughed, opened his arms, gesturing, 'what can I do' like I was some kind of fucking idiot.

"Bollocks to this I've had enough, you're not teaching me, I'm going to get some lessons," I shouted, throwing my seat belt off so hard it bounced off the window with a loud crack.

"Oi, you be careful," he warned.

"Bollocks, I don't need this, I'm going to get some proper lessons," I said, scrabbling out of the car.

Once I was out of the car, I slammed the door behind me, closing the chapter on this nightmare for good.

"Oh yeah, well, I'm not bloody paying for them!" He shouted in my wake.

I marched back into the house, found mum in the kitchen sitting at the table, she took one look at my face, she knew, she said in a weary tone, "Oh god, what happened?"

"I'm not going out with him again," I spat, "He's a bloody nightmare, I was doing fine, and then Mrs. Harrington comes along, you know how she drives, she must have been during about ten miles per hour and, he shat himself, grabbed the steering wheel, we nearly went up the kerb, onto the pavement, he's bloody useless Mum."

I chucked a tea bag into a cup destructively, grabbed the kettle up.

Into the kitchen pounds the old man, red-faced, angry. He sat down heavily.

"Oh well, that was a dead loss, wasn't it?" To one or both of us.

Mum sighed and asked, "What happened, Pudge?"

"I'll tell you what bloody happened, alright, he didn't listen to a bloody thing I told him."

"OK, OK, OK," Mum replied trying to calm him down.

"It was a total waste of time, I don't know if I want to take him out again, if he carries on like that, he'll do the car permanent damage."

I span around, "I told you I'm not bloody well coming out with you again."

"Oh yes, yes, you quit school, you quit your jobs and, now you're quitting driving, you're a quitter that's what you are, a quitter, a bloody quitter," he spat back.

I shouted, "I'm not quitting driving, I'm just not coming out with you again."

"If you'd just listen to what people said for once, you might learn something, but you won't though, will you? I think it must be all that crap you put on your hair; it's got in your ears, blocked them up," he said, grinning at his razor-sharp wit.

Mum laughed, the old man was encouraged, he went on, "Ah yes that's what it is, all that stuff on your hair it's got into your ears... Cloth ears."

"Oh fuck off," I told him.

Mum gaped at me, "Now, stop that, Mike."

"And you can piss off too," I said, it was out, before I could stop it.

In a second, the whole atmosphere changed; an isolating coldness crept in around me, engulfed me. I was alone, on my own, and apart from the steady humming of the fridge in the corner by the kitchen door, it was silent, a silence that was filled with shock, shock and menace.

"Now you listen to me sonny boy," said the old man, pointing his signet ring finger at me, "You can talk to me like that, believe me, I've had a lot worse, but you don't talk to your mother like that ever, you apologise... NOW!"

I looked down, away from the accusing finger, "I'm
not apologising, both of you can piss off, I've had enough of this
bullshit."

"You either apologise to your mother or we go outside, and then
you'll be for it!"

"I'm not apologising, and I'm not going outside."

"Oh yeah, we'll see about that, tough guy," said the old man, sitting
forward hawk-like steadily scrutinising me, waiting to pounce.

Mum pleaded, "OK, OK, come on, let's all calm down now."

The old man spun, "SHUT UP, YOU KEEP OUT OF THIS!"

"LEAVE HER ALONE, YOU'RE ALWAYS SHOUTING AT
HER!" I exploded, jumping up.

"Oh yeah come on then big man," he said standing, balling his fists.

Mum shot up too and cried, "STOP IT, STOP IT, STOP IT,
the both of you, stop it, I'm going out of my mind, I'm going
INSANE, I CAN'T TAKE IT ANYMORE!"

"No, nor can I… YOU CAN BOTH FUCK OFF!" I shouted,
before storming out. Smashing the kitchen door home, I took two
steps at a time on the way upstairs, threw open my bedroom door,
and slammed it shut on them, them, and their bullshit.

In the sanctuary, I chucked myself down onto my bed, turned over,
looked up at the blank ceiling, a blank canvas, my mind began filling

it in, replaying it all, trying to make sense of it all. It was obvious, I shouldn't have gone out with him in the first place. It was a stupid thing to do; he was a nightmare at breakfast. If we had gone out last night when he was in a better mood, it might have been alright, but whatever he had heard on the news this morning, combined with the electricity bill had got to him, and by then it was too late for me to back out. I didn't know, maybe, he felt pressurised trying to teach me to drive. One thing I did know was I shouldn't have sworn at mum, like that. It was wrong, I hoped she hadn't taken it to heart. I certainly didn't want her to piss off, she was OK she was, had time for people, had time for me. She was probably the sanest person in the house, I thought, grinning to myself. It was him. Why is he like he is? Why is he so negative? Why does he have to make everything so bloody complicated? Why does everything get to him so much? One chance we have at life, and even before his heart has stopped beating, he's already dead, the silly old sod. 'You're like a virgin with her first hot cock' he said, 'come on then tough guy' he said, 'outside', he said 'you'll be for it' he said.

In amongst it all, all the angst, the pain, the confusion, the fear that lurks inside. From the dark recesses, another memory, the one I tried not to think about, came festering to the surface. I tried to force it back down, think it away, thinking of something else, think of anything else, anything but that, there was no stopping it though, it was here now, rising up on a wave of red mist.

*

I was nine years old; my best friend Kevin Green had come around for me, the old man had answered the door and seen part of our door number was missing,

"What's happened to this? Where's that gone?" He said, pointing to what was left of it, turning on me.

I shrugged my shoulders, looked to Kev, he shrugged back, and we started looking for it.

Kev took a couple of steps out onto our grass, plucked up a small piece of black plastic.

"Is this it, Mr. Baker?" He asked, happily.

"Yes, it is," he said, turning it over in his hands. "Well, that's strange... How did you know it was there? Did you break it when you rang our doorbell just now?" He asked, looking down, his eyes boring into Kev's face.

Kev flinched, his face turned red, "No," he said nervously.

"You went straight to it; how did you know it was there? It was you, wasn't it?"

"It wasn't Dad," I interjected, defending my friend.

"So how did he know it was there then?" He demanded, irritably, in my direction.

"I don't know, Dad!" I cried.

He looked back at Kev, who was on the verge of tears now, "Well I bloody do, I'm going to have a word with your parents Kevin, come on," and marched off in the direction of Kev's house, with us following close behind.

On the way up to Kev's house, we found it hard to keep up with the old man's long, unwavering strides, but I wasn't going to give up. I was at his heels, half running, telling him it wasn't Kev. Kev was my best friend, he wouldn't do something like that; the old man's mind was made up though, he was going to get to the bottom of this one way or another.

Once we got up to Kev's house, Kev bolted up his garden path, frantically banged on the front door, and as soon as his mum answered it, he ran in, got behind her.

"Kevin? What's...?" She asked, her face a picture of confusion.

"Mrs. Green!" The old man accused.

"Oh, hello Mr. Baker, how are you?" She asked, looking up.

"Yes, yes, hello, no, not good I'm afraid, I believe Kevin snapped off our house number, and threw it on our grass, at the front of our house."

"Oh no, really? No... snapped off your door number, you say? No, I don't think Kevin would do anything like that, would you Kevin?" She said, looking down at her son cowering behind her house coat, "Did you do it, Kevin?"

He just about managed to shake his head.

"Please, Dad, he didn't do it!" I pleaded.

He was convinced though. "He walked out onto my grass and just picked it up, he knew exactly where it was!" He said, raising his voice.

Kev's mum folded her arms defensively, "I don't know, it's not something he'd normally do, did you see him do it?"

"Er... Well, no I didn't, he knew exactly where it was on my grass, he went straight to it, how did he know where it was then, you tell me that?"

Kev's mum's face clouded over; she'd had enough of this rude man standing on her doorstep making accusations about her son, "I don't know Mr. Baker, you didn't see him do it, you've got no proof, no evidence, it was probably just luck, or bad luck in his case."

I thought, yes, it was Dad, that's it; it was just bad luck Dad; this is the most embarrassing thing that has ever happened to me in my life, Kev's mum's right. "Yes, it was bad luck, you've got no evidence," I said, trying to sound like one of those tough American cops, Dad and me watched on TV when I was allowed to stay up late.

Kev's mum nodded her head conclusively, at last hearing something sensible,

"You've got no proof that Kevin did anything,"

I repeated, "Yes, you've got no evidence."

Kevin smiled through his tears, I felt encouraged.

"You've got no evidence."

"You've got no evidence..."

"... Kojak."

Kev's mum sniggered at the insult, sniggered at the bald-headed man with silly accusations.

"What did you say?" spat the old man, glaring down at me.

I repeated, "I said. You've. Got. No. Evidence. Kojak."

Kev's mum laughed; Kev laughed.

"Now you stop that Michael, I'm trying to sort this out," he said, his eyes flashing a warning.

I thought no, no I'm not, I'm cheering up Kev, I don't like to see him crying, you're wrong Dad, wrong,

"OK, Kojak, who loves ya baby?" I laughed, pretending to lick a lollipop.

Kev and his mum cracked up laughing.

"I think it's all been a big misunderstanding, Mr. Baker," Kev's mum concluded, now finished with this silly conversation.

"Hey Crocker get in here," I grinned, finishing my repertoire of Kojak quotes.

"I will talk to Kevin about it later," said Kev's mum, moving back into her hallway, fighting another big laugh that was welling up inside her. "Come on, Kevin," she said.

"I'm not happy about this, believe you me," said the old man, as the door slammed in his face. "I'll be watching out for him the next time he comes around," he said, raising his voice at the plywood door. "AND ANYONE ELSE WHO COMES AROUND MY HOUSE, I'LL CATCH YOU AND YOU'LL BE FOR IT, I'LL TELL YOU THAT FOR NOTHING!" He shouted into the estate.

I thought, it's over now, Kev's going to be alright now, everything's going to alright now.

"I'm going home now," said the old man coldly, looking down on me.

I nodded, smiled now that it was over, and followed him, but he was walking even faster now, big, long steps. So I had to run to keep up with him.

Dad and me liked Tom and Jerry. It was nearly five o'clock; Tom and Jerry time. Dad always said that once Tom had done something bad to Jerry it was OK for Jerry to do bad things to Tom, but sometimes he didn't though. Jerry did bad things to Tom anyway, and we both felt sorry for Tom the cat. Dad would say, 'Oh no, poor Tom, that was unnecessary', and we would both hope that Jerry the mouse lost. He never did, though.

"Dad, Dad, Dad, can we watch TV when we get home? ...Dad?" I asked.

The old man snorted.

On the relief road at the side of our house, under the cover of the ash trees, brambles, and stinging nettles, he turned and grabbed me viciously by the hair.

"You bastard, that cow was smirking at me," He snarled, pulling me backwards, forwards, forwards and backwards, sending excruciating pain ripping through me skull.

"You little bastard!"

"I'm sorry Dad!" I pleaded

"OH, YOU BLOODY WELL WILL BE!" He shouted, losing his grip, taking a kick at me as I tried to escape his ripping hands.

I managed to get two steps, but he was straight on me, his hand wrenched at the roots of my hair, lifting me off the ground, his feet kicking at my flailing frame.

"PLEASE STOP DAD!" I shouted to no one.

Once we got back to the house, he dragged me in through the back door, startling George who rushed past me making his escape, as I collapsed onto the tiled chess board floor.

"You bastard!" He screamed and disappeared into the garage.

I ran through the kitchen, and upstairs to my bedroom, slamming the door behind me, hoping that would be the end of it.
In the middle of the room, I stood, shaking, crying, out of breath; my head throbbing, scalp stinging, not knowing what to do, where to go, where to run to now, where to hide.

On the other side of the closed door, a storm of footsteps pounded up the stairs shaking the floor beneath me, with nowhere to run, nowhere to hide, I stayed in the middle of the room, alone, panting, and felt the warmth of urine cascading down the inside of my leg, soiling me. I waited, watching the door, I didn't have to wait long, the door flew open, and the old man came in brandishing the thick end of my mum's fishing rod. He didn't hesitate, he smashed me hard across my thigh, the pain knocking me helplessly down onto the floor, beneath him. Another hit to the back of my head had me balling up, rolling left then right, trying to dodge the assault, but the blows reigned down with impunity, raking every part of me, until I gave up.

Weary now, I lay still, accepting the punishment, accepting the deluge. It couldn't go on for much longer, could it? Surely, I would be dead soon; wouldn't I?

"OK, right, that's fixed you," he snarled and pounded out, slamming the door behind him.

In my bedroom, it was silent, cold isolation. I lay balled up on the floor shaking, praying, praying he would not come back again. If he did, I knew I couldn't take anymore, my head screamed, my body a maze of pain, a wetness on my legs? I checked for blood; it was the piss, seeping. Soiling. I had wet myself like a baby; I wanted my mummy; I cried for her, I called her, longed for her healing embrace, but it was all in vain though, she wasn't here, she was in hospital, wouldn't be back for another week. It may as well have been a lifetime.

I felt cold on the floor, wet, clammy, shaken, splintered. I had to move. So steeling myself, I slowly moved my broken body, got up onto the bed, folded myself into a ball, held myself tightly, watching as the daylight drained away, and the darkness flooded in around me.

I'm not sure how long I lay there, balled up, grizzling, shivering, it must have been hours though, as it was pitch black in the room by the time, I felt the first pangs of hunger in my stomach. I couldn't stay there any longer, I had to go downstairs some time, face him, and if there was more to come, then let's get it over with, surely the fear of the next attack was worse than the actual attack. I raised myself off my bed, ventured downstairs into the kitchen, where I found my older brother Martin buttering some toast.

"Oh, here is he, bubba Michelle, Dad told me, you just got wooled. DAD, DAD HE'S DOWNSTAIRS, HE JUST GOT WOOLED!" He shouted.

Martin cocked his head to one side, listening, there was no reply though, but Martin didn't need any help. Never did, "Ooooohhh have you been crying, little Michelle?" He smirked, looking me up and down, laughed at the wreck of a kid.

Martin's eyes stopped on the front of my trousers, he squinted, focusing in.

"Errrrgh, have you pissed your pants?"

"I haven't, I haven't," I sobbed.

"Oh my god, you have, you've pissed yourself, the little rat righteousness has pissed himself," he taunted, his voice full of joy.

"Nooo. Nooo!"

"I'm going to tell everyone."

"I didn't!"

Martin's face cracked up, "You're going to get eaten alive at secondary school, you are."

"I won't!"

"What's that poxy little song that you wrote? Oh yeah, 'I love kitten George, he is so lovely, he purrs when I stroke him, he's as happy as can be'. Dee, dee, dee, YOU FUCKING POOF!"

"SHUT UP, SHUT UP, SHUT UUUUUUPPPPPPPPPP!"

A surge of pure anger bought me back to the present. I was on my bed back in 1983, it couldn't touch me. I pushed it down, buried it all over again, deeper this time. It really was a matter of survival; it was either eat it up, or be eaten by it, and I knew with my temper, if I had let it, dwelled on it, it would have eaten me up inside. It was simple, live or die. In the years that followed, I had reasoned it away. I had worked out why the old man had done it. The worry of mum being ill, far away in hospital. Martin spending all of our food money for my mum's three-week stay on fags and sweets for his mates at the local shop, then the humiliation of two young coppers pulling him up for speeding on a visit to mum in hospital, lecturing him in front of his kids, making him look small. On top of it all, the worry that this time, he might be the one being made redundant from his job, as the Tories boom and bust economic policies came back around to the inevitable bust; breaking Britain, breaking the very voters who swept them to power in the first place. "Kojak" had been the final straw for him, the old man had just snapped. It was no excuse, but I couldn't live with that kind of hate, the ticking time bombs that we all carry around with us from day to day, pushing them down smothering them; the unwanted offspring of being victimized had to be dealt with. So, what did I do? I buried it along with all the other childhood shit that had me reaching for the razor blade, cutting at my slender white arms, bloodletting, before Pete O'Shea and punk rock had come along and given me some hope.

I couldn't think about it anymore, so I got up, went back downstairs, opened the kitchen door, half hoping he was in there, so I could tell him to fuck off again. Only to find Mum sitting at the table, alone, head in her hands; my heart broke open.

Mum slowly looked up at me, her eyes wide, "Mike?"

"I'm sorry, mum," I said sadly, my voice full of remorse.

She nodded, "I know you are."

I sat down, putting my hands flat on the table and exhaled deeply, "He just does my head in."

"Yes, believe me, I know, I've had a few years of it now," she sighed.

"Why is he like he is, why does he rant all the time?"

"Oh, it's a long story Mike, he wasn't like that when I first met him, he was a nice man, he liked to dance and have fun, he's just old and tired now."

I sighed, I hadn't really thought about him as a youngster, what he was like, what he liked.

"I thought he was the bees' knees, when I first met him, he was such an intelligent man, very knowledgeable, practical too, could fix anything electrical, he knew a lot about the world, he had seen most of it in the Merchant Navy, it's sad, but the world he knew has gone now, he just doesn't understand it anymore, everything's different now."

I nodded, trying to understand.

"Did you know he was born in Edge Hill in Liverpool in the 1920s?"

"No, was that bad then?"

"Boy oh boy, terrible it was Mike, he was born in a place they called pig muck square, it was between the gas works and a pig market. He told me, that depending on the direction of the wind, you'd either smell the pig shit or be gassed to death by the leaky gas containers, he was lucky to survive a lot of kids didn't make it, TB killed most of them. George your Granddad, suffered from shell shock after WW1, spent time in a mental institute, so when Dad was sixteen, he had to go out and work, went to sea on one of the trawlers out of Liverpool docks, then the war came, and he joined up, he joined The Merchant Navy, went on the North Atlantic conveys, he saw some of his friend's ships go down right in front of him, it was tough, he got hit with shrapnel himself, he's had a hard life, don't judge him too harshly."

I nodded again, it sounded like a hard life, but I still couldn't work out why he took it out on us. On anybody, in fact, how could ranting and raving change your past? It couldn't, the past was exactly that, the past, and if it was that bad, then bury it.

Mum beamed a radiant smile, satisfied in the knowledge that one day I might understand, see beyond my own morals and see it from another point of view.

"I think we should book some driving lessons, what do you think?" She told me, drawing a line under it as far as she was concerned.

"I'm not sure mum, maybe I should give him another try, what could possibly go wrong?" I laughed.

Mum laughed at her son's easy going way, shining her light onto me, "You can always laugh, Mike, and believe me that's a good thing in this world, I can tell you."

I smiled back into the light. "Yeah... I think it would be safer for everyone if we booked some driving lessons," I said getting up,

"Thanks Mum, I'm going out, I'll see you later."

"See you later," she said standing herself.

"And Mike... don't worry about Dad, I'll have a word with him, he'll come around."

"Thanks Mum," I replied, grabbing my leather jacket, leaving through the back door.

On the way past the front of our house, I saw the lounge light flooding out onto the rose bushes under the window. He's in there now, I thought, probably watching the news, probably getting angry about something he has no control over all over again, well that's up to him. I needed to take control of my life, learning to drive could help, maybe get a job too, it looked like I might not have a choice in that matter, now, with or without Mum and the old man's constant barracking. I needed to concentrate on the band too, there had been too many distractions, too much energy used on non-band related matters. I thought we'd been on our way; thought I was invincible, not only as a decent punk guitarist, but as an avenging angel. When I strutted into Dawkins place to rob him, of not only a few of bottles of whiskey, but to shake the wanker up.

In the weeks since Cannon and Ball had descended on us for that botched burglary, it seemed like everything had gone wrong. I had made every mistake known to man. It was the starting point which led to the waste of time job interview, driving with the old man, the almost fight, the digging up of things better left buried. Kissing Hayley and telling Dave her brother and my best mate about it, wasn't the brightest thing I've ever done either, and there was Stampy and Moley lurking in the back of my mind, to worry about too.

A million stars shone above me as I walked down my road past the Harrington's house, the oak tree, onwards towards the white fences that divided Doggy's house with the vicarage, and I wondered why out of all of them, all those different stars and planets, Stampy and Moley had to be on the same one as me. Mathematically I reasoned, it must be millions to one, but reality didn't do maths, maths was just another way we measured things, to make sense of the chaos.

I had heard the rumours, not surprisingly, after I gave them, the wankers sign on the bus in Ware that day. They were after me, they had been seen around Ware a few times since.

Stampy, and Moley and other members of The Wolf Pack had been heard in the Tap asking questions about Punks in Ware, especially 'a ginger cunt who lives in Thundridge'. Stampy and Glen Mathews had approached a rattling Dirty Den in the high street a few days later to say that they wanted 'a word with Whiff too'; maybe they thought it was open season on punks. I didn't know, but when I told Whiff about the rumours, he had laughed it off, but I knew it bothered him though; he didn't want to feel that kind of pain again as the blood-red D.M.s hit home.

In between the white fences at the bottom of my road I walked, Doggy's house on the right, dark, tomblike as usual at night. Hilary's to the left, every light blazing, every curtain drawn, like it always was, day or night. I shook my head, smiled to myself, thinking the bloke was a complete nutter, carried on walking towards the end of the fences, the first crosses of the graveyard revealing themselves to me, silhouetted in the distant orange glow of the A10.

A scream of pure anguish rang out from the grounds at the front of the vicarage. I stopped, froze, listening intently. It sounded like a cry from a baby. A baby in pain, a baby in desperate need of attention. Surely, it couldn't be a baby I thought, could it? Hilary's mental health hadn't improved over the years since Dave and me had taken his motor for a spin. If anything, it had got a lot worse, but human sacrifice no. Not even he was that mental. Was he?

"Who's that? Where are you?" I whispered into the darkness, tilting my head to one side, tuning in, trying to locate the source of the cry

"Eeeeoooowwwww," came back to me from the gloom.

Oh what, it's some kind of animal, I thought, obviously trapped, certainly terrified, definitely in a lot of pain, I can't just leave it, I've got to try to help it. I bent down, looked through the slats into Hilary's front garden, and saw a fridge had joined the other detritus from the day before; it's pearly white surface reflecting back at me in the lights from the house.

On the other side of the scorched lawn, past the lit up fridge, I made out a low hedge. It waved frantically in my direction, then stilled, then whatever was inside let out another desperate cry.

"Eeeeeeeeooowwww"

I knew if Hilary caught me on his property, I was more than likely to be smited in a fever of religious retribution, but I had to find out what was going on. It such a desperate plea.

"I'm coming, just hold on little one," I cooed, trying to reassure it.

One step at a time I carefully edged out onto the patchy scorched grass, dodging around the fridge, a rusty statue of the Buddha, and a Corby trouser press. Crunching over other unseen objects beneath my D.M.s I tentatively made my way up to the source of the noise.

"Eeeeeooooowwww", said, the waving bush frantically.

In amongst the branches of the bush, low down, I could just about make out a white cat, a white cat like Doggy's cat Faustus. Oh, shit it is Faustus, I thought, and he's chewing at his paw, like he's trying to bite it off. Bloody hell. I've got to help him. Got to help him now.

I rushed forwards, the Good Samaritan, and went straight over an old TV set, and as I smashed down onto the scored earth the cathode ray tube imploded beneath me with a dull thump.

"Fucking hell," I said, to no one, sitting up dusting flecks of glass off my bondage trousers.

Once I had got most of the glass off, I renewed my rescue attempt. Only this time, moving slowly forward, watching the ground for any more hazards. I tentatively made my way over to the bush, drew back the branches and there was Faustus trapped, a piece of string wound around his front paw. I pulled at the string. It wasn't going anywhere, at its end, it was tied to a chisel that had been firmly knocked into the ground. Oh what, it's a fucking snare, I thought, a snare! Why is he in a snare? Oh, yeah Hilary. OK, let me see if I can release it. So taking the taut string in my right hand I gave it another tug and as it closed tighter on Faustus' paw, he went crazy, clamping himself onto my leg like a bear trap, teeth biting, puncturing holes in my leg.

"Ahhh Jesus, get off, I'm trying to help you, you little twat," I hissed, lifting my leg up, trying to shake off his vice-like grip.

"Who are you?" Came a voice from behind me.

Malcolm, Hilary's boy, stalked out of the shadows.

"Malcolm, bloody hell, don't do that, you scared the shit out of me," I said, hopping up and down, still trying to get the wretched cat off my leg.

"I said, who are you?" He demanded.

"Who am I? I'm Skinner you fucking knobend, Skinner from up the road," I said, swotting at the limpet like cat, with an open hand.

"Oh, are you? Well, if I was you Skimmer, I would get out of my garden."

"What! Shut up, you little turd, ouch, fucking hell, get offffff," I said, hopping up and down.

"Don't make me hurt you," he said, advancing on me.

"Who put this snare here?" I asked, ignoring the twerp.

"I did, and I'll do what I blooming well like in my garden, it's my garden."

"NOW GET OUT OF MY GARDEN, NOW!" He shouted, putting up his fists.

One more shake of my leg and the string broke, pinged off into the darkness, releasing one extremely traumatised cat and seeing his chance. He bolted, jumping over the TV set and out the garden, disappearing under the pampas grass, at the front of Doggy's house.

"Ahh that's better, what a relief... Bloody hell that stings," I said, rubbing at my leg, tracing the punctures with my fingers.

"I SAID GET OUT OF MY RUDDY GARDEN!" Shouted Malcolm, who was now bopping and weaving like a Victorian boxer.

"Oh, piss off you little wanker, I'll get off your oooooff."

I felt an effeminate blow connect with my cheek; it would have been a poor punch for a six-year-old, let alone an eleven-year-old.

"Ha, and there's plenty more where that came from," he said, feigning a couple of jabs.

"I'm warning you, Malcolm."

A small white fist like a chicken leg swept harmlessly past my ear, followed by another lame slap on my other cheek.

"I mean it Malcolm, back off you little turd, one more…"

"Ha, ha you coward, had enough, have you?" He said triumphantly, leaping up like a gazelle.

I sniffed, scratched my cheek, took aim and booted him so hard in the bollocks that he lifted a foot off the ground.

"Aaaaahhhhh!" He said.

When he landed again, he dropped to his knees, lurched forwards, mouth gaping, trying to suck every bit of air off the planet.

"I'll get off your property now," I said, stepping back from the prone kid, "And if I catch you setting snares again, I'll put you in one, you little shit."

A moment later, a door flew open at the side of the house, letting the light inside, flood out onto the scuffed grass around us and the gargantuan silhouette of Tamara thundered towards us.

"Malky, Malky, Malky, oh my little Malky, what happened?"

Malcolm sobbed, "Mummy, mummy, mummy, he hit me, I went for a walk, I didn't do anything, he, he hit meeeeee," pulling himself into Tamara's humongous balloon like breasts.

"Oh what, leave it out, don't lie. Mrs. Charman, he came at me like Jo Bugner, he hit me first."

"NO, No, no, I couldn't, I turned the other cheek, like Jesus, and he punched it," he cried frantically, engulfing himself.

"Shut up, stop lying, did you know he's been putting snares in your front garden?"

"What utter rot, snares in the garden! He wouldn't do such a thing, would you, my darling Malky? Malky, my little Malky, what's he done to you?"

"Mummy, he hurt thingy."

"Oh, you beast, you beast, you beast. You, fibber. You Satan in safety pins," cried Tamara, shielding her youngster, from the devil himself, her eyes full of a mother's fortitude.

Malcolm nestled in, "Booby milk, mummy, booby milk mummy, mummy."

"Shhh, shhhhsh not now my dear, later my little lamb, later," she whispered.

I stood, stunned, eyes unblinking, trying not to let the image in. It got in.

"Euuugh, fuck this, I'm off," I said, turning my back on the horror show. "Booby? Milk? Oh, you dirty bastard".

On my way back across the scorched grass, I took my anger out on the stricken TV, kicking it, showering glass everywhere, and then stamped onto the driveway, heading for the white fences. I felt a chill run down my spine, someone or something was close by, an earthly presence, watching me, analysing my ever move, stopping, turning, I saw there on the bonnet of Hilary's car, the boss-eyed cat. One eye on me, studying, taking everything in, one eye on the heavens above like he was transmitting his findings back. I cringed, sped up, and got the hell off their property, entered the white fences, watching, waiting for some kind of super wrath from Hilary the head nutcase of Nutcaseville. He never came though, it was all quiet on the God front, and once I had vaulted the wall into the graveyard, I felt safe, it was over; for now, anyway.

Inside the graveyard, it was silent, the dead lay rotting in their plots, their final resting places, while the cold stones above, their markers, threw out their familiar shadows in the orange glow of the A10. Inside my head, it was a totally different story, though, booby milk. Booby milk! Mrs. Charman breastfeeding Malcolm her eleven-year-old son; Milkies for Malky. I didn't know whether to laugh or puke up. In the end I decided to laugh, my braying laughter echoing around the stones, off the mausoleum, with its ominous ten-foot-high Celtic cross, which held no fear for me anymore. I had already seen a vision of hell tonight, everything seemed ordinary now.

I felt a chill as I plodded through the tired grey stones, spring seemed a long way off today, winter still gripping on with everything it had. I zipped up my leather jacket, to keep it a bay, thinking Dave is not going to believe this one, it's better than anything else we've heard from the vicarage. Booby milk. Milkies for Malky. I smiled, walked on down the hill, saw the flood of lights blazing from the all-night garage, I smiled again at a memory, stones reigning down on cars, then next to it, Dave's house lit up, friendly homely, inviting. I opened the gate, wandered under the car port, into the kitchen where Dave greeted me with a curt nod and immediately walked out, and as he walked out, Hayley walked in, with a thunderous look on her face.

"I knew you'd tell him, you arsehole," she spat, turned and slammed the door behind her, leaving me alone, in the silence of the kitchen.

Dave re-appeared.

"You told her?"

"She's my sister, mate," he said, shrugging his shoulders.

I shook my head, unbelievingly, "I can't believe you told her, Dave!"

"I'm sorry, Skin I'm always going to put her first, aren't I...? She's family mate, she's blood, it's all about family, isn't it?"

I stood looking at him for ages, trying to comprehend, trying to figure out what to do next, what to say next, we had been mates for years. He steadily held my gaze, not looking angry, he wasn't going to back down though, not when it was about his family.

"I mean seriously, Skin, what would you have done if it was your sister?"

I looked down, I knew alright, I would have done the same thing he did in his situation, maybe worse if I had a sister, even a free spirited one like Hayley.

"You understand, don't you? You gave me no choice, mate."

I exhaled deeply, nodded, finally conceded, "Yeah I understand, look Dave, I'm going now mate, I haven't had the best of days, seriously."

Dave nodded sympathetically, followed me out under the car port, then smiling broadly he said, "I wouldn't worry about it, Skin, she'll forgive you."

I thought oh yeah good one mate, well done, you know that's not what I'm bothered about at the moment, I couldn't be bothered, just shook my head at the audacity of his comment. "I'll see you tomorrow then, Skin?" Dave asked, like it was a question.

"Yeah of course… See you tomorrow, Dave."

On the way back up the hill to the graveyard, I ran it all back in my mind, trying to straighten it out, it didn't take long. Of course Dave had told her, deep down, I always knew he would. One thing about Dave was, you could have a laugh with him about most things, but when it came to family though, that was his red line. You passed over it, he would say something. No matter who you were, mate or not, and it was the right thing to do, to protect the people closest to you.

I wondered why I didn't have the same kind of loyalty for mine, they were my blood after all, then I thought of my brother, the sick bully boy punching his frustrations out on his little brother, five years his junior. The old man distant, lost in a world of politics, flaying hopelessly at the ghost like images on our black and white TV, then there was mum, poor mum. A positive beacon of hope, the life raft keeping the Baker household afloat. It had been particularly tough on her, this family life. A dreamer. A gentle soul, left to work out situations that she was ill-equipped to deal with. She was tired now, fed up with it all, taking on water, drowning in it, and as I weaved my way through the broken headstones of the graveyard I looked down into the cold grey granite and thought maybe death might not be such a bad thing after all.

In the early hours, of the next morning I got up, went straight down to Dave's, to catch him before he went to work. I didn't mess about. He was right, so I apologised to him unconditionally, telling him I really didn't know what had happened that night with Hayley and me and in true Dave style he replied, 'No, nor me mate, nor me,' like it was one of life's biggest mysteries, before laughing his head off.

"It's a shame, Dave, I would have been a decent brother-in-law," I said, hoping now, that the tension was gone or nearly gone.

Dave laughed back catching it, hoping too, "I know mate, can you imagine the old man though," and he Alan-ed, "Bloody hell Hayley, you're marrying Baker? Have a heart mate," and we both fell about laughing, the tension was truly gone.

"I better go Skin," he said, hearing Alan tooting his horn from the all-night garage forecourt.

"Cheers, Dave," I said, putting my hand out.

"Bloody hell, leave it out Skin, you'll have me misting up like some old granny," he said, giving my hand a cursory shake.

Dave and me said our goodbyes, parting on good terms, which is what I had hoped for. It was the first of the many bridges I thought needed to repair. Second on the list was the old man. It was to take a lot longer with him, though. His wife had been insulted, and he had not only been abused, he had also been challenged as the man of the house. Deep down he was a sensitive kind of man, took things to heart, which was probably one of the reasons for the way he was. In the days that followed, we ate in silence, avoided each other during the day and then on the third day, I walked into the front room and found him sitting in his rocking chair warming himself by the bar fire. One bar on, TV switched off, paper folded neatly on his lap. I didn't know what to expect, and was thinking of walking out again, so I was surprised and not just a little bit relieved when he spoke to me, I couldn't do a long protracted war of attrition.

"Hi Mike, what you up to?"

"Oh, nothing really, I'm probably going out later," I said, guardedly.

He set the paper down, "Mum says you're going to have some driving lessons."

I thought oh no, here we go again, "Yeah?" I asked challengingly, waiting for it.

"I think that's a good idea, I never took a driving test in my life, so I'm probably not the best person to teach you... You know something, if I took the test now, I don't think I'd pass."

"Hmmm, you reckon?" I said, struck dumb, nodding mechanically.

"Yes, so, look Mike, here's the deal, if... Or should I say, when you pass the test, you can have the Mini, it's not in the best shape, but it would be a good first car for you, I was thinking of getting something new anyway, so what do you say?"

"Yeah OK, brilliant, thanks Dad!"

He stood up, reached forward, "Shake on it?"

I took his hand. It was a firm shake, we shook for a long while, two men who had found a solution to their problems and as he let go of my hand, he moved to hug me, but pulled away at the last moment, his generation didn't do that kind of thing, that was for the women to do.

A smile for his son was followed by a seat next to the bar fire. He flipped the switch to give himself another bar of heat, grabbed his magic zapper, pushed the red button, giving the TV life, bringing the world into our front room. While I strode out, feeling like a huge weight had been lifted from my shoulders and now, finally, I could concentrate on the most important thing of all.

Virus V1's next gig.

Printed in Great Britain
by Amazon